Case Studies

Managing Key, Strategic, and Global Customers

Noel Capon

Christoph Senn

Library of Congress Cataloging-in-Publication Data

Capon, Noel
  Case Studies in Managing Key, Strategic, and Global Customers / Noel Capon with Christoph Senn
    p. cm.
    ISBN: 978-0-9833300-6-6
      1. Strategic Accounts—Managing. I. Title: Case Studies in Managing Key, Strategic, and Global Customers.
II. Noel Capon / Christoph Senn

Editor: Noel Capon
Design/Cover Design: Anna Botelho

Foreword

In recent years, many corporations large and small, based in many countries around the world, have developed key, strategic, and global account management programs. Correspondingly, business schools, consulting organizations, and the Strategic Account Management Association (SAMA) offer courses for practicing managers. Additionally, business schools provide courses for graduate and undergraduate students, often supplementing courses on sales management and personal selling.

To some extent, these courses suffer from a lack of cases studies of real-life account management situations. This volume is an attempt to redress that situation. Some cases are traditional long-form cases; others are merely a single paragraph. Regardless, each case focuses on a particular account management issue. Some cases require extensive preparation; other cases can be assigned just a few minutes before class discussion.

This book is available in printed form and as a pdf e-book. We use print-on-demand technology. Hence, we anticipate updating the book from time-to-time with additional cases as they become available.

Also by Noel Capon

Key Account Management and Planning

Managing Global Accounts
with David Potter and Fred Schindler

Strategic Account Strategy

Sales Eats First
with Gary S. Tubridy

TABLE OF
Contents

Building Materials, Inc.

Jack Barnes was the newly appointed national accounts manager for Building Materials, Inc. (BMI). BMI was a major player in the U.S. construction industry. BMI supplied a wide variety of building materials to construction companies across the U.S. from factories in the southeast and California. BMI participated in both the home-building and commercial markets.

Historically, most construction in the U.S. was local. Local developers worked with local architects and local builders and construction firms. BMI had developed an effective sales organization to address this market. A national sales manager (NSM) reporting to the CEO directed this effort. The NSM's direct reports were eight regional managers (RSMs), each located in a geographic region. RSM's in turn directed several district sales managers (DSMs); each district sales manager supervised eight to ten salespeople.

Over the years, BMI had an enviable profit record; even in economic downturns BMI generally managed to squeeze out a small profit. BMI was known for quality products but industry observers attributed much of its success to sales force management. Top management set aggressive goals but provided significant rewards for meeting sales and profit targets; conversely, it did not hesitate to fire sales managers and salespeople who did not perform to expectations. Successful salespeople and sales managers earned bonuses and commissions that made their take-home pay above industry averages.

In recent years, BMI's sales organization had come under some pressure. Some developers, construction firms, builders, and architects were expanding beyond their home bases. Some operated regionally; others had become national firms. Whereas these firms had previously discussed projects and/or purchased materials locally, increasingly they operated more centrally, including purchasing at regional and/or national offices. Top management became aware of this trend when BMI lost several projects with long-time customers.

In an attempt to address the problem, BMI hired Jack Barnes as national accounts manager (NAM) from another building products firm, reporting to the NSM. In his first meeting after being hired the CEO told him: "Jack, we have a growing problem and we want you to solve it. We've had a very successful system in the past and it still works for our local customers. Don't make any dramatic moves; get started by figuring out the lay of the land. But I want to see a plan for change in three months time. Good luck."

Anglo-India

Anglo-India was a major global construction firm with an excellent reputation and exceptionally strong financials. Mostly its customers were developers that contracted Anglo-India to construct new buildings to designs their architects developed. Sometimes Anglo-India was involved in the design phase. When Anglo-India bid on a potential project it made a detailed cost analysis, then added around a three percent fee for completing the construction. Generally, Anglo-India and its competitors developed very similar cost estimates. When there were numerous potential projects, Anglo-India's fee was greater than three percent; when projects were more rare and price competition became widespread, Anglo-India's fee would be as low as two percent. In most contracts, Anglo-India negotiated a cost saving formula. If project managers were able to identify cost savings, Anglo-India and the client would share in the proceeds. Anglo-India's senior managers wondered if there were opportunities to improve its ability to win business from competitors.

Two upcoming projects were a hospital addition whose main component was several additional operating theaters, and a hotel project for a well-known brand that employed a franchise model. The hotel company planned to build the hotel, then sell to an investor group that would finance the purchase with some equity but significant debt.

Jeremy Edwards

Collins, Inc. was a Connecticut-based producer of precision parts for many U.S.-based firms. Collins was well known in the industry for its high quality products and excellent service. Typically, Collins was able to extract a price premium from customers that valued the benefits it delivered. One such customer was ABC Inc. Jeremy Edwards was Collins's strategic account manager at ABC.

For many years, Collins's business had grown steadily; a few years previously it reached $25 million annually, but had since dropped to about $15 million, and was continuing to decline. Despite Jeremy's best efforts, he was unable to halt the slide. ABC's procurement managers told Jeremy that Ting Won, a Chinese manufacturer, was delivering products that almost matched Collins's quality; that was sufficient for a significant part of ABC's product line, hence the reduction in Collins's business.

Upon further investigation, Jeremy discovered that ABC's orders spiked at various times during the year. His contacts within ABC told him that Ting Won sometimes had delivery problems. On those occasions, ABC ordered from Collins on an emergency basis. Jeremy wondered if there was a way he could use this information to modify Collins's relationship with ABC.

Contact Inc.

Contact Inc. was the market leader supplying a wide variety of stationary products to office product superstore chains like Staples, Office Max, and Office Depot – its strategic accounts. Contact had one major branded competitor with a similar product line; it also competed with its strategic accounts' private-label products. Each superstore chain was increasingly seeking to differentiate itself from competitors via private-label brands. As a result, they gave increasing shelf space to private labels in their plan-o-grams. Another problem for Contact was that each superstore had full information on sales and profit margins for all products it sold, but these data were not available to Contact (or its branded competitors).

With existing products, Contact was sometimes able to use 3rd party awareness and usage studies, SKU ranking reports, and product testing to demonstrate its products should receive additional shelf space. This process was more difficult for new products where Contact had limited sales history; it had to rely on packaging, testing, and trade marketing plans.

Contact's executives wondered what options were available for what they saw as an ominous trend.

Ohio, Inc.

Ohio Inc. was a market leader; its products were used in many manufacturing operations. Since inception many years earlier, Ohio sold to industrial distributors that in turn sold to many types of manufacturers. Industrial distributors maintained inventory of many product varieties and offered fast customer delivery. Ohio had a network of exclusive distributors that it treated as strategic accounts; its two major competitors had similar arrangements with their own distributors.

Ohio also had strategic relationships with several large end-user customers for product development; they purchased new products from Ohio's distributors. These firms previously purchased large quantities of Ohio products but had shifted to lower-price suppliers. For several years, some of these firms had asked Ohio to serve them directly, believing that dealing directly with the manufacturer would allow them to gain some of the distributors' margins in lower prices. Ohio rejected these requests because of long-standing relationships with industrial distributors

Ohio's distribution decision caused its relationship with large end-user customers to continue to atrophy. For established products, end-user customers increasingly purchased directly from smaller firms; Ohio's sales volume continued to drop. Ohio faced no such problem from smaller end users; they continued to purchase from its distributors.

Ohio's executives were increasingly concerned with the loss of business at large accounts. They wondered what actions to take.

Rudi Thomas

Rudi Thomas was an account manager for Chemsol, a European chemical company; Rudi's global customer was Physco. Chemsol manufactured and sold *panogane* to Physco as a raw material for its production process. Because *panogane* was dangerous to manufacture, Chemsol developed *panogane** (modified form of *panogane*) using a different but much safer process.

Based on extensive technical analysis, Chemsol and Physco technologists demonstrated that *panogane** was equivalent to *panogane* as a raw material for its production process. Physco's manufacturing personnel were also convinced despite a generalized concern with changing something that was working well from Physco's perspective. Chemsol was also able to demonstrate improved product attributes for *panogane**, and more efficient manufacturing for Chemsol. Since Chemsol would pass on efficiency savings to Physco of several million dollars annually, a switch to *panogane** would be financially beneficial for Physco. Chemsol also told Physco that its major competitor had already made the change.

Notwithstanding the value that Chemsol offered Physco and the effort that technologists from both firms had expended, Physco did not agree to make the switch. Rudi wondered why.

Software Consulting Inc.

Software Consulting Inc. (SCI) was a large software consulting organization providing implementation expertise to clients that purchased complex software solutions from major software providers like SAS and Oracle. Initially, SCI worked mainly with small- to mid-size companies. Account managers (AMs), paid largely on commission, were responsible for following up leads and securing new business. When a client signed a contract, SCI appointed a project manager to take charge of implementation using a combination of SCI and client personnel; implementations could run for a few days to a few weeks. SCI believed its model for implementation with small to mid-size clients was highly effective.

In recent years, technological advances and increased functionality allowed SCI to penetrate *Fortune* 100 companies. Implementation cycles were longer and clients required additional services; in general, they were increasingly dissatisfied with SCI's service and lack of communication. To address this problem, SCI appointed engagement managers (EMs) to oversee activities at large clients.

EMs were supposed to help alleviate communication and deployment issues. Specific responsibilities included new client sales support, client management, resource deployment, and up-sell of services. Although EMs achieved some success, problems remained.

The most serious issue concerned account responsibility and communication with the account. Because large accounts had the potential to be major revenue drivers for SCI, senior partners often visited these accounts independently of the EMs; communication with the EMs about these visits was spotty. AMs secured large firms as customers, often for a limited initial engagement, but they continued to work in the account trying to identify new opportunities. A typical EM might manage three or four project managers, but was also supposed to be expanding SCI's business at the account. Finally, client personnel often asked project managers if their expertise could add value in other business units.

SCI management was concerned that its lack of focus could leave it vulnerable to competitive threats from Accenture, Deloitte Consulting, and IBM.

Jack Adams

Jack Adams worked as a global account manager for Travel, Inc., a large U.S-based provider of global travel services. Jack's single customer was Consulting, Inc., a major global provider of consulting services based in London. Travel, Inc. was organized into eight product divisions and four geographic areas – North America; Latin America; Europe, Middle East and Africa (EMEA); and Asia Pacific (APac). Jack was responsible for the entire Consulting, Inc. relationship. He reported directly to Travel, Inc.'s general manager for Great Britain, and dotted line to a global account director in Travel's corporate office. Although Jack had revenue responsibility, Travel's P&L statements ran though the geographic regions; the product divisions also had P&L targets.

In recent months, Jack believed he was receiving insufficient support from one Product Division President and the Regional VP for Asia Pacific. Agreements made with Consulting, Inc.'s corporate office were not being properly implemented in either the product division or Asia Pacific. Jack's major internal contacts were with product-marketing heads and individual country managers; all contacts told Jack they were giving as much attention to Consulting, Inc. as possible. Jack sensed these organizations did not consider Consulting, Inc. a top priority. He was also having difficulty with his direct supervisor in securing budget for an extended Asia-Pacific trip to address the issues in person.

Jack was unsure how to proceed. One option was to bring in his executive sponsor (ES) for Consulting, Inc., but he was unsure how effective this would be even if the ES confirmed his suspicions. A New York-based colleague, who was also a global account manager, had intimated that she was having similar problems. Jack wondered if he should discuss the possibility of a systemic problem with the global account director.

Martin Schleicher

Electron Inc. was a major producer of household electronics products like TVs, DVRs, and other audio and video systems. Electron's products were available in most countries around the world and its brand name was well known. In recent years, some retail customers like Walmart (U.S.) and Carrefour (France) had expanded regionally or globally. Electron had made organizational changes to address these evolving strategies, notably by appointing regional and global account managers.

Martin Schleicher was Electron's account manger for Palfrey, a major retail chain with aggressive international expansion plans. Electron was Palrey's major supplier overall, but its position varied country by country. Schleicher spent a significant amount of time at Palfrey's headquarters working with global procurement and other departments that were driving Palfrey's expansion. One of Schleicher's challenges was to construct promotion plans that Palfrey would implement in various country markets at the individual store level. Negotiations were long an arduous but Schleicher reached an arrangement whereby Palfrey would receive a four percent rebate on its purchases from Electron if its reached agreed sales targets. Senior managers at both Electron and Palfrey were pleased with this arrangement.

Two months into the promotion plan period, Schleicher discovered that Palfrey's implementation was spotty. After speaking with several Electron and Palfrey executives in various countries, he learned about a competing promotion plan offered by Positron Inc, one of Electron's major global competitors. Structurally, the Positron plan was similar to Electron's – four percent rebate if sales reached a target level – but Positron made its agreements with Palfrey's individual countries rather that with the corporate group. The various targets in the Electron and Positron plans were comparable. Palfrey also learned that at least one of Palfrey's country managers had decided not to implement Electron's program.

Schleicher wondered how he should proceed.

Janet Marsden

Janet Marsden was a U.S.-based Strategic Account Manager (SAM) at Tech Inc., an important supplier of communications equipment to leading firms in many industries globally; one of her three customers was Portia, a strong regional bank in the Eastern U.S. Janet had formed an excellent relationship with Portia. Tech had the best product range, the best service, and the best prices. For several years, Portia had placed 99 percent of its requirements with Tech Inc, making it effectively a sole-source supplier.

Portia was a wholly owned subsidiary of European-based Iberia Bank and historically made sourcing decisions independent of its owner. However, Janet learned that Iberia had decided to integrate Portia more closely into its growing U.S. operations. (Tech Inc. was a minor Iberia supplier in Europe.) For the time being, Portia would continue to make its own procurement decisions for communications equipment, but Iberia required that Portia adhere to its procurement policies. Notably, Iberia strongly pursued a dual-vendor strategy.

Transforming Procurement at Merck:
Beyond Purchase Management[1]

In June 2005, Bill Gibson, Director of Sales, General Motors (GM) Fleet and Commercial Operations, was considering a Request for Proposal (RFP) to supply fleet vehicles to Merck & Co., the $22 billion pharmaceutical company. GM was sole supplier to Merck's Canada operations and provided high-end vehicles to Merck's senior executives. However, for the past eight years, Ford Motor Company (Ford) had supplied the bulk of Merck's U.S. fleet while GM had bid unsuccessfully every single year. Gibson knew that the new 2006 RFP was fundamentally different. Merck aimed to consolidate its entire western hemisphere fleet requirement with one supplier. As he considered his bidding strategy, Gibson examined what had changed at Merck during the previous year.

FLEET VEHICLE SUPPLIERS

Although the retail automotive market was extremely competitive with many suppliers, the fleet market had different characteristics. Fewer manufacturers actively competed, in part because some suppliers had insufficient capacity to ensure timely delivery to large fleets such as Merck's. For example, Japanese manufacturers (Nissan, Toyota, Honda) and Volkswagen managed their capacities to supply the more profitable retail market. However, for active participants, the fleet business provided volume *to load their capacity*, as well as a *test-drive* opportunities for potential future sales. Major fleet suppliers in the Western Hemisphere were primarily DaimlerChrysler, Ford and GM. Each had automobile models compatible with Merck's requirements. In model year 2006, the Big Three together were planning to launch five new fleet vehicles, more than in any of the previous 20 years.

Overall in 2005, the situation for the Big Three U.S. automakers was discouraging; they continued to lose market share mainly to Asian producers while simultaneously earning low margins. Ford had announced plans to improve its cost structure by closing plants and reducing its workforce. It was also trying to boost profit margins by increasing retail sales and paring sales to fleet customers (around 32 percent of total sales), especially to car rental companies that earned large discounts for bulk buying.

Market share loss was anticipated, but analysts believed that Ford was moving to use fleet sales as a kind of safety valve to manage extra production capacity, not a large, sustained business. Merck's current U.S. fleet vehicle was the Ford Taurus, soon to be replaced in

11

Ford's line up by the Fusion. Compared to the annual 400,000 Taurus production, planned annual production for the Fusion was 250,000 units.

GM remained the overall market leader but was continuing to lose share. Analysts believed that GM would have to close plants, reduce workforce, and resolve legacy cost issues (including renegotiating union contracts to reduce healthcare cost for retirees) in its bid to turnaround its business. In the short run, GM had sufficient cash ($19.8 billion in the first quarter of 2005) and adequate credit lines; it could also raise additional cash from its profitable GMAC unit. Fleet sales represented 25.9 percent of GM's 2005 U.S. sales. GM had announced that it would focus on fleet sales, but would also increase prices for the car rental business to improve profit margins. DaimlerChrysler had engineered somewhat of a turnaround by reducing capacity and launching successful new models. Analysts did not expect it to drastically increase discounts on its fleet vehicles during the next three years; rather it was pursuing a margin raising strategy.

MERCK'S AUTOMOBILE REQUIREMENTS

Merck was among the ten largest fleet owners in the world. It operated approximately 12,800 cars in its three western hemisphere regions (U.S., Canada and Latin America) mainly for field-based sales and research employees to make physician office visits and distribute samples. Most fleet cars had a life of 65,000 miles (roughly three to four years) for an annual replacement requirement of 3,000 to 4,000 vehicles. Each region purchased locally for a 2003 spend of $66.5 million. In the U.S, Ford was Merck's primary supplier with an annual contract; GM was the sole supplier in Canada with a multi-year contract; Merck had several suppliers in Latin America. (See Exhibits 1A and 1B for details on Merck's supplier base, volume, and pricing.)

MERCK BACKGROUND

From being a Wall Street darling during most of the 1990s, in the early 2000s, Merck was somewhat of a whipping boy in the business press. "Any day you come in and the mouse is frowning, it's not a good day," was how Richard Clark, CEO of Merck, known as a numbers man, humorously summed up the problems his firm had been facing. During 2004, Merck had been making the headlines for its unproductive new product pipeline and growing legal battles over liability lawsuits for its arthritis drug, Vioxx, which it voluntarily withdrew in September 2004. Analysts speculated Merck would be critically wounded for years to come by costly court battles with thousands of former Vioxx users, eventually having to pay them billions of dollars in damages. In addition, Merck faced the impending patent expiration on its $5 billion anti-cholesterolemic drug, Zocor, in June 2006.

During its 115-year U.S. history, Merck developed a highly entrenched corporate culture — *The Merck Way*. Loyalty was valued, employees viewed stability as a strength, and a *not-invented-here* (NIH) syndrome was rampant. During decades of solid growth and profitability, R&D, marketing, and sales were Merck's competitive advantage as they developed and successfully marketed a stream of blockbuster drugs. As a result, Merck conducted much of its operations in silos, where a drug team might have its own dedicated marketing and sales personnel. It wasn't at all unusual for a single physician to be visited by multiple Merck sales reps, each promoting a different drug, on the same day.

Though many deemed Clark merely a caretaker CEO when he took charge in May 2005, under his direction Merck put a long-term plan in place to regain profitability and growth. In part Clark extended a culture change initiative that he started while previously serving as President of Merck Manufacturing Division (MMD). An important element in Clark's approach was evolving Merck's culture and organization structure to drive quicker, fact-based decision making, and streamlining the way products moved from R&D to commercialization and product launch. One of his first culture-change actions was transforming the Procurement function. Rising operational costs with flat revenues were unacceptable (Exhibit 2). In 2003, Clark agreed to a plan for saving $1.2 billion on procurement spending from 2004-2008. If fully successful, the impact would be equivalent to an 11% earnings per share (EPS) increase on the 2003 base. In 2004, Merck's annual procurement spend was $ 7.26 billion.

INDUSTRY BACKGROUND

The U.S. was the world's largest pharmaceutical (Pharma) market and Pharma was its most profitable industry between 1995 and 2002. In 2003, lack of new products, third-party payers' hard line against price increases for patented drugs, and patent expiration, generic competition, and price erosion caused its fall to third place; in 2005, it declined further. Analysts estimated it would end the year in fifth place, with a net profit-to-sales ratio of about 16%, versus 6% for all *Fortune* 500 companies. Although very respectable compared to most manufacturing industries, this performance was a far cry from the 1990s (Exhibit 3). In general, R&D-based drug companies had high operating margins (operating profits as a percentage of sales); these were considered necessary to fund new R&D and absorb product liability risks — in the early 1990s, 40% ratios were not uncommon among leading drug makers, but had contracted to 25% to 30%, However, they were still around three times the average of the S&P 500.

Historically, Pharma rejuvenated itself by developing premium-priced breakthrough therapies that opened up entirely new markets. However, the current dearth of new products was leading firms to restructure and/or seek alliances or deals. An added problem was the pressure that Pharma faced for its pricing practices. A research study by AARP (an advocacy group for Americans aged 50 and older) found that manufacturer prices were increasing at more than triple the general inflation rate. Managed care organizations (MCOs), concerned about rising health expenses, were vigorously trying to contain their pharmaceutical costs. As a result, Pharma firms were trying to rationalize their cost structures.

THE PROCUREMENT FUNCTION AT MERCK

Merck had manufacturing and sales operations in 54 countries; the Procurement function was a sub-division under Manufacturing. Each of Merck's 31 manufacturing sites had its own independent site team that coordinated procurement for that particular plant. The site team's role was to assure continuous supply of raw materials and packaging and procure local service needs; aside from assuring continuous supply, it was not considered a critical organizational function. The Global Procurement function performed centralized procurement services for individual business units. While attempting to service the business needs of its stakeholders in the individual business units, it had no power or remit to implement procurement practices across business units or to champion joint buying by multiple manufacturing sites. Economies of scale were not frequently leveraged and there was no official system for sharing best practices.

From a human resource perspective, procurement jobs were often one element in a Merck manager's job rotation. A three-year appointment to gain commercial experience was common before moving onto another job. As a result, the procurement organizations did not generally develop deep functional expertise. As head of MMD, Clark saw significant opportunity to consolidate and rationalize procurement costs as a key means to deliver the cost savings required to meet his division's profit targets. As former head of Merck's pharmacy benefit management business, Medco (previously spun off), Clark understood the discipline of being cost conscious in a low margin business; his goal was to bring a similar discipline to Pharma, historically a high margin business.

One of Clark's first actions was to bring in procurement expertise from the outside. In January 2004, he hired GlaxoSmithKline's (GSK) Procurement head Willie Deese. Deese had transformed procurement into a global function at SmithKline Beecham, and subsequently repeated the efforts at GSK when SmithKline Beecham merged with Glaxo Wellcome. Deese joined Merck on the condition that he be given freedom to drive transformational change. His task would match nicely with Clark's goal of revamping Merck's production and supply network to use more external sources of supply. Merck was highly vertically integrated and certain parts of the system had relatively low capacity utilization rates; Clark believed that these areas were cost ineffective.

Deese had the unenviable task of first making sense of the processes and complex structure that was the Procurement function at Merck. Procurement was a loose alliance of individual site procurement departments under the Business Units, and a centralized procurement function that was not well aligned to consolidate the needs of business units or sites. Business Unit Heads had budgets for external spend, but their performance was tied to achieving targets rather than saving money. They had little incentive to explore cost savings either within their business units or in concert with sister businesses.

An important feature of Deese's approach was collaboration. He did not intend Global Procurement (GP) to control expenditures. He believed such an approach would become dysfunctional because customer needs would become secondary to cost control. He firmly believed that GP's customers, the business units, should define their needs; then GP's job was to find the most cost effective solution to meet those needs. Deese believed that GP should, however, control the sourcing process as a vehicle to manage expenditures.

Deese also had to reckon with internal resistance to change. He said, "Corporate initiatives were optional at Merck." Since GP did not control spending budgets of the business units it supported, it had to work with senior leadership and business unit heads to effect change. Since budget owners were line managers, influencing them was another primary challenge; the prevailing attitude was: "it's my budget and I'll do what I think fit." In dealing with such managerial conservatism, Deese was helped by Merck's three years of flat revenues and some late-stage disappointments with new products coming out of Merck Research Labs (MRL). Then, with Vioxx's withdrawal, the procurement transformation effort was launched in earnest. Merck's executive committee asked the business units to build in $124 million in 2005 budget cuts into their profit plans, derived from procurement savings.

TARGETS

Because raw material costs were a small percentage of COGS and operating margins were substantial, traditionally procurement received little attention at Merck. Although its peer companies had similar economics, Pfizer, Wyeth, GSK, Novartis, and Bristol-Myers Squibb each had much more effective processes; recently, they had been issuing guidance statements to Wall Street for cost reduction strategies with procurement contributions. Merck's Procurement function was one of the least integrated in the industry. In top Pharma companies, spend per procurement professional was around of $15-20 million per year; at Merck, the results varied greatly across the organization and were often much lower (Exhibit 4). Also, Merck's procurement function typically saved approximately $105 million per year — 1.4% of total annual spend; other Pharma companies had cost savings of 4-5% per annum.

At Merck, GP only influenced 52% of the approximate $7.4 billion projected annual spend, but even here it could not effect significant change. Procurement had no influence whatsoever on 48% of spending — healthcare benefits, legal, management consulting, car fleets or on high degrees of spend outside the U.S.; the respective business units and corporate functions independently managed these. Procurement would have to rapidly extend its influence on external spend from the current 52% level to 90% by 2007 if it was to achieve its savings commitment targets.

An early task was to try to understand Merck's spending patterns. All spending was categorized based on geography: local — single continent, single country; regional — single continent, multiple countries; international – from 2 to 4 continents, multiple countries; and global — more than 4 continents, multiple countries. Deese believed that the current mix was not optimal; the distribution was too heavily skewed in the local direction. Human resources – recruiting, pensions, healthcare benefits, and the like was an extreme example. Merck had more than 63,000 employees operating in 54 countries; local spend was 91% of the total, and procurement was involved with only 15% of this spend. An early goal was to raise spend management to a higher level of geographic consolidation (Exhibit 5) to better leverage Merck's global footprint and implement rigorous sourcing processes to each spending category. Viewed a different way, spending categories were raw material/PPE (Plant, Property & Equipment) – 30%; SG&A – 50%; and R&D – 20 %. SG&A and R&D related spend of 70% were the low hanging fruit to be targeted first.

When Deese felt he had a handle on the scope of the job he set about working with Merck leadership to secure its buy-in and sponsorship of the work. He aimed to demonstrate that Procurement could realize substantial cost savings for the business units; these savings could be returned to shareholders, or re-invested in R&D, marketing and sales efforts to drive revenue growth. He anticipated supplier resistance and employees' unwillingness to change suppliers, but his core argument was potential net dollar savings and successful implementation at many other companies. He argued that Merck was at a distinct competitive disadvantage. Merck's Management Committee and MMD leadership agreed and the Operational Excellence group allocated budget funds for the change effort. These funds were to be paid back that same year together with incremental savings.

EARLY EFFORTS

Faced with the need to institute new ways of working and ramp up procurement skill levels, Deese engaged QP Group, a consultant firm to jumpstart the process and validate the savings opportunity. He then committed to a five-year plan to save $1.2 billion in expense and capital spend in 2004 – 2008, as well as offsetting all inflationary effects. The first-year operations savings goal was $138 million; the year 2 goal was $270 million. Deese also engaged Exegy, a supplier of contract procurement professionals, to bolster Merck's bench strength and attack previously non-procurement spending categories. QP and Exegy trained all Procurement employees in a new five-step Sourcing Management Process (SMP) and implemented a plan to launch *waves* of cross-functional teams to attack various spending categories. Deese also restructured his Global Procurement Management Committee (GPMC) comprising leaders of the Procurement function. The GPMC was responsible for managing procurement, its employees, and meeting savings targets. In the early stages, the GPMC suffered from the stigma of procurement's historically restricted role within Merck.

To expand its sphere of influence within Merck, GP set out to change the relationship with the supply base. It faced two major challenges:

1. Many of the supplier relationships were entrenched because of heritage, and supplier changes were difficult to execute; and,

2. GP had limited influence over many of these supplier relationships.

Deese believed Merck's historically fat margins had made it price insensitive; hence it paid a premium for goods and services. High prices might be justified for specialty chemicals in drug development but not for packaging supplies, bulk chemicals, employee benefits, and car fleet management, to name a few spending areas. Procurement teams discovered that many supplier relationships had been in place for 20 to 30 years. They consistently charged different prices to different customers for the same product or service and invariably they billed Pharma clients higher.

Deese organized a series of Supplier Forums to align internal Merck executives and senior supplier executives to the changing expectations for business and commercial relationships. In June 2004, Merck met with its 100 top direct material suppliers; one month later it met with its top 100 indirect suppliers of services. (Merck held a third forum in London for its top 100 European suppliers in January 2005.) At these forums, Deese told suppliers about Merck's difficult business climate, its strategy for change and cost control, and challenged them to present plans to bring down their costs to Merck by 20% over three years. Deese reinforced this challenge by asking for white papers on how each supplier could help Merck achieve its required cost savings. He sought to create a sense of partnership and to shift away from relationships based on history. Cost-saving targets were 7 percent immediately in year 1, 7 percent in year 2, and 6 percent in year 3. Deese asked for immediate savings in the form of refunds or rebates; in turn Merck would implement the supplier's white paper. Deese also asked Merck executive stakeholders to reinforce to suppliers that Merck was going to follow through with real supplier changes, based on performance.

By end July 2004, as the first white papers were coming in, the GPMC informed Deese they would fall $7 million short of the 2004 savings target of $138 million. Further, there was no defined activity pipeline to meet the $270 million target for 2005. As Deese's reputation for never failing to meet a target was at risk, he ratcheted up the effort by placing a renewed emphasis on change management, cross-functional collaboration with other business support functions, and bolstering his procurement team by recruiting outside talent.

To kick-start the effort, in July 2004, Deese hired Howard Richman from GSK to oversee the change process and be his chief of staff. Richman was previously a member of Deese's GSK procurement team and had been through the entire Procurement transformational cycle. Other strategic hires made by early 2005 were: Richard Spoor (GE and Nokia) as VP Indirect Procurement (eventual leader of the Procurement function); Sara Todd (Wyeth) as Executive Director European (EMEA) Procurement region; Mark Scheftel (Booz Allen and IBM) to manage major indirect spend categories previously not under Procurement; and Patti Whitehouse (Bank of America) to run the Learning and Development activities necessary to build a world class Procurement function. GPMC now had a breadth of global, external, and leadership experience that had not previously existed in the paternalistic Merck environment.

Deese also formed an extended GPMC to supplement the GPMC's work and help with change management activities. The extended GPMC, chaired by Richman, included representatives of other business support functions:

- Finance: to define what constituted savings; validating and tracking savings; monitoring budgets; Human Resources: to assess employee skill levels; develop job descriptions for new roles based on the new required skill sets; compensation planning; recruiting new and diverse talent; training; determining staffing requirements to support the function;

- Legal: establishing new templates for contracting activities; support for contract negotiations in categories not previously under Procurement's responsibility;

- IT: systems and data support for Procurement; and,

- Public Affairs: to help run a communications plan and campaign to align Merck employees to the changes, the new ways of working, and the successes achieved.

THE TRANSFORMATION PROCESS

An early task of the GPMC to affect change and establish credibility was to publish the Savings Rule Book. (See Exhibit 6 for a sample page.) The rulebook specified the procedures for classifying, approving, and rigorously documenting all savings. Functional/divisional finance managers had the responsibility of signing off on achieved savings. The MMD Finance group conducted a second level of financial review for all savings in excess of $1 million. Savings categories in decreasing order of importance were:

- Absolute cost reduction from price last paid

- Cost reduction compared to market for new products

- Cost reduction versus budget

Only actual cost reduction counted toward savings; cost avoidance (like offsetting inflation or avoiding penalty payments) did not. The purpose of the rulebook process was to establish credibility and alignment for the cost saving activity. Eventually cost reduction would become part and parcel of the budgetary planning processes. In addition to the Savings Rule

Book, Merck built the Global Procurement transformation process on four pillars; a new Sourcing Management Process (SMP), People development; Expense management, and Supplier management.

PILLAR ONE: SOURCING MANAGEMENT PROCESS

Merck designed its new Sourcing Management Process (SMP) (July 2004) to address complex business purchasing challenges. The objective was to deliver quick wins that would build momentum, and develop medium- to long-term sourcing strategies. These would leverage Merck's global footprint and produce a step change in procurement performance. Merck executed the SMP via empowered, cross-functional teams sponsored by major business unit stakeholders. The five-stage process and tool kit comprised:

- Stage 1. Define business requirements (AQSCI) based on: A - Assurance of Supply, Q - Quality/Regulatory needs; S - Service levels; C - Cost; and I - Innovation. Merck set these priorities in diminishing order. AQS had absolute thresholds, C was scalable; Merck incorporated I if required. Merck would never sacrifice necessary levels of AQS for Cost or Innovation. AQSCI was the backbone of the entire procurement process;

- Stage 2. Gathering and analyzing internal and external market data;

- Stage 3. Generating strategic options leading to innovation and breakthrough sourcing approaches;

- Stage 4. Executing the strategy, usually by bidding or negotiating contracts; and,

- Stage 5. Launching continuous improvement plans for measurable, long-term sustainable impact.

Specifically, SMP sought to:

- Provide a concise business problem solving tool that could be uniformly applied on a global scale;

- Enable stakeholders and sponsors to understand the procurement challenge faced, and bring forth new breakthrough solutions; and,

- Provide Sourcing Managers and/or teams with the purpose, direction, and executive sponsorship needed to start and run the process.

An SMP process began when a Global Procurement Sourcing Manager, assigned a category of spend, lined up an Executive Sponsor (typically the functional head where the budget spend originated) and formed a cross-functional team with representation by all key stakeholders. The team adopted a Project Charter, a seminal document representing the authority that the sponsor vested in the team to work on the sourcing category. The charter sought to answer questions regarding the goal and purpose of forming a sourcing team for this category of spend, the role of each team member, and the responsibility boundaries. The Charter also served as a check on the team's work at regular intervals and was used to measure progress against the original intent.

Once the Project Charter was in place, the team developed an overall plan and key steps in the form of a road map (Exhibit 7). With the plan in hand, Procurement undertook a portfolio analysis to determine what approach to take to the specific sourcing challenge (Exhibit 8). It analyzed the segment and prioritized the total portfolio of spend according to required cross-functional involvement.

The portfolio chart comprised two dimensions: relative value/profit impact and market risk/complexity. Position on the relative value/profit impact dimension was based on the spend's business impact, its risk-return profile, competence of team members, and the certainty and stability of that spend for that business requirement. Position on the market risk/complexity dimension was assessed based on internal complexity--level of stakeholder' confidence in the procurement process and Procurement's involvement and access to spend, and external complexity—based on the product/service being outsourced, the nature of existing supplier relationships, the number and strength of individual suppliers in that category, and Procurement's ability to impact the spend.

A companywide portfolio analysis of spending categories yielded the following broad metrics that GP used as general guidelines for 90% of Merck's spend:

- Just do it — 40%: These categories were a small percentage of the total spend and supplier power was low. Procurement bought on the organization's behalf with minimal stakeholder involvement.

- Collaborative Fast Track — 30%: In these categories the sourcing process was more complex and suppliers might have substantial power. Procurement worked with smaller, *ad-hoc* teams to help achieve savings and secure value-added services.

- Joint Strategic Sourcing — 30%: These categories were a large percentage of total spend, with moderate to high sourcing complexity. Procurement led cross-functional teams including all stakeholders to create a strategy for leveraging purchases across Merck.

For each spending category, Sourcing Managers identified the stakeholders — anyone who might be affected by the strategy review, and anyone who could influence/impact the strategy development or implementation process. The fundamental job for stakeholders was to define the AQSCI business requirements (Stage 1). These requirements formed the basis for creating and evaluating options, identifying the final strategy, and measuring implementation success.

In Stage 2, sourcing teams collected facts and data about the current supply situation via supplier analysis and market research. Data on the existing supplier base included supplier sales volume, product range, spend as percentage of supplier sales, value of products/services by supplier, number of orders per supplier, performance and relationship history, current supplier contract data and expiry dates, financial ratios, investment plans, ownership structure, and directors' interests. Teams looked beyond current boundaries for new supply opportunities. They considered substitute products, current suppliers' competitors, and new developments in the relevant supply market, including small diverse businesses.

In Stage 3, teams conducted a value chain analysis of the sourced product/service based on costs and benefits. They delineated suppliers' cost structures to determine both floor and ceiling prices for use in negotiations; in general, procurement teams had a better understanding of suppliers' costs than the suppliers themselves! A team would produce a Source

Plan — an actionable document for that sourcing category (Exhibit 9). The plan would be approved by the sponsor and signed off by major stakeholders. Source plans helped in contract negotiations and yielded significant cost reductions.

In Stage 4, executing the strategy, the procurement team assessed and mapped the scale of change — supplier change, product/service change or modification, and level of stakeholder involvement. In supplier management, Stage 5, Merck pursued a planned method for driving continuous improvement. This process included supplier forums and a formal Supplier Value Management (SVM) program.

PILLAR TWO: PEOPLE

Executing SMP and leading cross-functional teams required a very different skill set from the old regime. Performance requirements from Sourcing Managers and leaders were also very different. The Procurement function required a critical mass of managers with both procurement process skills and subject matter expertise to attack the many categories of spend that previously were not Procurement's responsibility. The GPMC and HR developed a skills assessment inventory of all current Procurement employees. They held 90-minute interviews to assess competency against critical skills needed to run SMPs. Skill gaps were identified and closed via training programs. For some employees, skill gaps could not be closed and they exited the function or the company.

Merck also conducted an intensive six-month recruiting effort to add 50 people in the U.S. and 10 in Europe. It targeted individuals who had successfully performed in similar SMP roles with other companies, together with high potential, trainable talent from other functions at Merck. More than 200 candidates were interviewed. Merck developed targeted onboarding processes to ensure that new employees were quickly assimilated, trained, and received guidance in Merck procedures, rules, regulations and systems. Also, 150 Procurement personnel at Merck's manufacturing sites reporting into MMD site managers were re-assigned to the Procurement function and trained in SMP.

There was also significant change at the top of the Procurement function. In May 2005, Richard Clark was promoted from President MMD to become Merck's CEO. Willie Deese replaced Clark as President MMD, and Richard Spoor, previously in charge of expanding Procurement's role into unconventional spending categories was named head of Global Procurement. Spoor was now responsible for delivering the $1.2 billion, 5-year savings commitment that was promised to the street. Howard Richman assumed Spoor's responsibilities, and Patti Whitehouse took on the added responsibility for change management, replacing Richman. Rounding out the GPMC were Dan Nardi, a 25-year Merck professional as head of MMD and Capital Procurement; Andy Shigo, a 15-year Merck professional as head of Research Procurement; Sara Todd, head of EMEA (Europe, Mid-East, Africa) Procurement; Marc Sylvestre, a 12-year Merck professional in the newly created position of head of Asia Pacific Procurement; and Courtland Butts, the Finance representative to the team.

PILLAR THREE: EXPENSE MANAGEMENT

Historically, Procurement activities focused mostly on price, terms, and purchase conditions; savings were gauged as reductions from last price paid. Procurement did not consider approaches that managed the total cost of ownership (capital plus ongoing maintenance expense), or opportunities to use less. As the new Procurement regime took hold, Merck started to use other approaches. These included using less expensive alternative goods or services, finding ways to use less by eliminating waste, and abolishing certain types of spend altogether.

Success in these new approaches often involved changing policy. Examples included: moving to a single travel policy for all business units; eliminating steps that created wasted effort; ensuring compliance with preferred provider contracts; standardization to reduce the number of items in a category and so optimize supply chain leverage. In part, these approaches surfaced from the white papers delivered by suppliers to meet Merck's 20% cost-reduction targets. To execute successfully required addressing significant internal complexity.

PILLAR FOUR: SUPPLIER MANAGEMENT

Forty percent of Merck's products relied heavily on third party partnerships; thirty percent of its total purchased spend was with 30 different suppliers. Many of its partnerships and supplier relationships had been in place for 20 to 30 years; this had bred complacency.

Following the 2004 Supplier Forums, Merck received 196 whitepapers — 181 from current suppliers, the balance from high potential suppliers looking to win its business. Merck quickly realized that many suppliers were far ahead of Merck in terms of procurement best practices. Some suppliers had access to their clients' learning curves in multiple industries; others had implemented their own process improvements. Suppliers collectively committed to $20 million in upfront rebates and payments as they signed up to the 20% challenge. The total potential value of savings indicated by the white papers, if fully implemented, was approximately $175 million. By mid 2005, $30 million of incremental value was created by implementing the supplier-generated ideas.

A commonly suggested improvement area was process rationalization. Suppliers knew that some of Merck's internal business processes promoted inefficiency and high costs. For example, color changes on drug packaging were expensive, cumbersome, and time consuming; they required authorization from several people, including the Medical Review Board. Relatedly, product managers often worked with creative agencies to produce branded promotion items like pens, notepads, charts, and memory sticks for salespeople to hand out as *reminders* to doctors and pharmacies. At one time, there were 200 different models of pens in use! Sourcing plans based on supplier whitepapers reduced the number of promotion items to one-to-two models per brand, with color and logo customized to individual brands. Merck consolidated production with a single supplier in China; average cost per item fell from $1 to 25 cents.

Henceforth, the nature of Merck's relationship with suppliers would be driven by the category of spend. Furthermore, Global Procurement and the business units and corporate functions would jointly share relationship ownership. For core and unique services, Merck implemented a higher level of scrutiny and management of the supplier relationship. Overall, partnerships with suppliers, rather than one-off transactions, would have the goal of securing greater cost discipline and strategic alignment over time. Because of the complex set of supplier and licensing relationships, involving several vertical and horizontal levels,

R&D operated differently from the rest of Merck. But even here, the procurement function staffed R&D projects with people who were qualified technically to represent the needs of Merck's research labs to the suppliers.

Going forward, high performing supplier relations would become a key value driver for Merck. Merck segmented suppliers on the basis of scale and importance of spend category. Merck would leverage some supplier relationships to secure the lowest possible costs; it would treat other suppliers as long-term strategic and deal with them more collaboratively. For example, Merck helped a contract dosage form development company with capital funding to expand its business. In another example, a packaging company and Merck jointly undertook a lean six-sigma initiative. Also, a Chinese based firm providing services to support new drug discovery partnered with Merck to roll out a fee-based program for conducting research.

Merck began to select suppliers based on accessibility, technological superiority, competitiveness, and global influence. Cost savings was a major selection criterion, but each supplier had to meet threshold criteria of assurance of supply, quality, and service. Suppliers that could deliver innovation were most favored. This was especially critical for advanced pharmaceutical ingredients (API), critical to drug development and manufacturing.

Merck discovered that many of the middle-tier suppliers were more willing to step up to the challenges it offered that bigger firms. Middle-tier suppliers were often more nimble than their larger counterparts — they often suffered from structural inefficiencies similar to those that had beset Merck. Many larger suppliers had a global footprint, but a lack of standardization made worldwide collaboration difficult and cumbersome. For example, Merck's supplier of bottle caps had facilities across the world, but its Asian capabilities did not match those in the U.S. Of course, if these large suppliers were able to restructure to meet Merck's needs, they could translate their learning to other clients.

PERFORMANCE ACHIEVEMENTS

By end 2004, Global Procurement had over 30 procurement teams in place and 130 procurement staff trained in the new sourcing methodology. It validated $172 million in fiscal year 2004 expense savings against a $138 million target, plus an additional $65 million in capital savings. Further, in 2005, it was anticipating $275 million in expense savings against a $270 million target. As a result of these efforts, the business units included $124 million savings into their 2005 budget assumptions.

As a way of building momentum for the procurement efforts, the GPMC used cash awards and other forms of recognition to motivate team members. Frequently circulated News Flashes helped communicate the early successes, share best practices, and recognize the cross-functional team efforts.

Merck also moved forward with a Supplier Diversity program for minority, woman and veteran-owned businesses. Historically Merck had operated a minimally funded effort to assure compliance with Federal Government regulations for large businesses that provided it with goods and services. In 2005, GP initiated a strategic effort to ramp up the existing level of 5% of U.S. spend with diverse suppliers to 10% by 2010. Because many of these suppliers are smaller and had lower overhead, they were often cost competitive, provided better service, and were faster growing. They also aligned with Merck's strategy of building a supply base that reflected the customer base for its products.

BACK TO GENERAL MOTORS

In his meetings with Merck Procurement managers, Bill Gibson, Director of Sales, General Motors Fleet and Commercial Operations had gained some insight into the transformation of the Procurement function at Merck. He wondered how these changes would affect GM's ability to secure significant business from Merck. Certainly, its approach to the new RFP had to be very different; if it were to win, GM would have to displace Ford, Merck's long-time car fleet supplier.

ENDNOTES

1 Sumitra Lastkarthikeyan provided research and writing assistance under Noel Capon's supervision. Howard Richman, Executive Director, Marketing and Commercial Services Procurement, provided significant insight into case events.

EXHIBIT 1A. VEHICLE PURCHASE VOLUME AND BUYING FREQUENCY

	Annual Purchase	Timing	Refresh Cycle
Canada	up to 200 vehicles	throughout year	3 years
USA	up to 3,100 vehicles	twice a year	3 years
Latin America	up to 650 vehicles	throughout year	3–4 years

EXHIBIT 1B. LATIN AMERICA FLEET SUPPLIERS

Country	Fleet Size		OEMs	# Units	
México	728	31%	Chevrolet	1,001	42%
Brazil	466	20%	Ford	283	12%
Puerto Rico	267	11%	Peugeot	199	8%
Argentina	206	9%	Toyota	151	6%
Venezuela	149	6%	Volkswagen	120	5%
Colombia	144	6%	Nissan	113	5%
Peru	111	5%	Renault	98	4%
Ecuador	92	4%	Honda	74	3%
Chile	82	3%	Mitsubishi	68	3%
Costa Rica	47	2%	Mazda	30	1%
Guatemala	24	1%	Fiat	29	1%
El Salvador	18	1%	Jeep	29	1%
Panama	16	1%	Citroen	25	1%
Honduras	13	1%	Hyundai	21	1%
Nicaragua	6	0%	Others	128	5%
	2,369	100%		2,369	100%

EXHIBIT 2. MERCK SUMMARY FINANCIALS (in $ mil. except per share amounts)

5 yr Balance Sheet	12/31/2006	12/31/2005	12/31/2004	12/31/2003*	12/31/2002
Total Assets	44,386.1	44,777.3	42,562.3	40,580.0	47,527.9
Total Liabilities	24,420.3	24,453.5	22,867.2	21,088.4	24,399.1
Shareholders' Equity	19,965.8	20,323.8	19,695.1	19,491.6	23,128.8
Total Liabilities and Shareholders' Equity	44,386.1	44,777.3	42,562.3	40,580.0	47,527.9

* Decrease in assets and shareholder's equity in 2003 primarily reflects the impact of the spinoff of Medco Health
Source: Merck Annual Report and Thomson ONE Financials

5 yr Income Statement[1]	12/31/2006	12/31/2005[2]	12/31/2004[2]	12/31/2003	12/31/2002
Net Sales or Revenues	22,636.0	22,011.9	22,938.6	22,485.9	21,445.8
Cost of Goods Sold	3,732.7	3,264.4	3,509.1	3,141.9	4,004.9
Depreciation, Depletion & Amortization	2,268.4	1,708.1	1,450.7	1,314.2	1,067.5
Gross Income	16,634.9	17,039.4	17,978.8	18,029.8	16,373.4
Selling, General & Admin. Expenses	12,948.3	10,984.8	10,381.0	9,378.0	8,329.4
Operating Income	3,686.6	6,054.6	7,597.8	8,651.8	8,044.0
Earnings before Interest and Taxes	4,422.6	6,154.1	7,414/2	9,097.0	9,651.7
Net Income	4,433.8	4,631.3	5,813.4	6,803.9	7,149.5

1 Excluding discontinued operations of Medco Health
2 Amounts in 2004 and 2005 include the impact of the withdrawal of Vioxx

Per Share Data	12/31/2006	12/31/2005	12/31/2004	12/31/2003	12/31/2002
EPS	2.03	2.1	2.61	3.03	3.14

EXHIBIT 3. THE PHARMA INDUSTRY — COMPARATIVE COMPANY ANALYSIS (Net Income ($ million) and Compound Growth Rate)

Company	2005	2004	2003	2002	2001	2000	1995	10-yr.	5-yr.	1-yr.
Bristol-Myers Squibb	2992	2378	3106	2034	2043	4096	1812	5.1	−6.1	25.8
Johnson & Johnson	10411	8509	7197	6597	5668	4800	2403	15.8	16.7	22.4
Eli Lilly	2002	1810	2561	2708	2809	3058	1307	4.4	−8.4	10.6
Merck	4631	5813	6831	7150	7282	6822	3335	3.3	−7.5	−20-3
Pfizer	8094	11332	1639	9181	7752	3718	1554	17.9	16.8	−28.6
Schering-Plough	269	−947	−92	1974	1943	2423	1053	−12.8	−35.6	NM
Wyeth	3656	1234	2051	4447	2285	−901	1680	8.1	NM	196.3
Astrazeneca	4706	3813	3036	2836	2967	2328	522	24.6	15.1	23.4
Aventis	NA	NA	2460	2282	1454	−27	678	NA	NA	NA
GlaxoSmithKline	8060	8247	8022	6333	4498	6296	1655	17.2	5.1	−2.3
Novartis	6130	5767	5016	5287	4232	4450	NA	NA	6.6	6.3

Source: Thomson ONE Financials

EXHIBIT 4. EMPLOYEE TO SPEND RATIO WITHIN PROCUREMENT IN 2004

	People	Total Spend $ million	Spend per person $ million
Group Global Procurement	176	3,764	21
Local Site Procurement	136	1,097	8
Non MMD Procurement	76	1,523	20
Not Visible 'Shadow Groups'	130	880	7

Source: Merck internal data

EXHIBIT 5. PROCUREMENT SPEND CATEGORIES

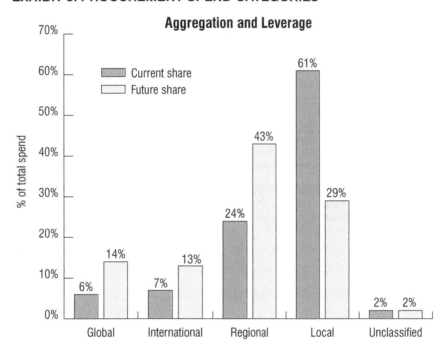

EXHIBIT 6. SAMPLE PAGE FROM THE SAVINGS RULE BOOK

PROCUREMENT SAVINGS DEFINITION

Procurement savings are measured and defined as an action taken by Procurement that results in a reduction against one of the following baselines;

1. Previous price paid

2. Internal proxy or relevant external pricing* (for goods or services not currently purchased)

3. Budget

Note: If #1 above does not exist, go to #2, then #3

- For service based contracts, where no previous unit price exists, use lowest competitive legitimate bid or best legitimate proposal as the relevant comparable pricing baseline.

- Effective in 2005, "Procurement Savings" will measure cash outflow savings related to expense <u>and</u> capital reductions. Avoidance savings and inflation allowance will not be included.

  – For **expense cost reductions**, savings can be claimed for the first 12 months after implementation of the initiative, and year-over-year cost reductions over the term of the agreement.

  – For **capital cost reductions**, savings can be claimed over the life of the capital project. Savings can only be applied to the year in which the capital expenditures occur.

- ***For areas of spend influenced by Procurement, the inability to offset price increases must result in the recording of negative savings.***

Note that it is the decision of each business unit whether Procurement savings will be used to reduce their budgets, or whether they will be used to increase purchase volume or re-invest in other parts of their business.

Source: Merck procurement savings handbook, Dec. 2004

EXHIBIT 7. KEY MEETINGS IN THE SOURCING MANAGEMENT PROCESS

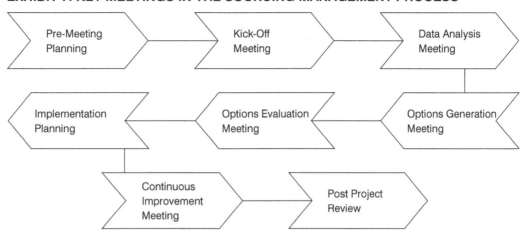

EXHIBIT 8. THE PROCUREMENT MATRIX

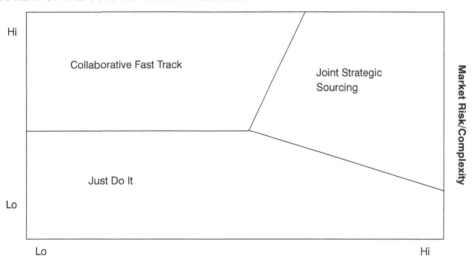

EXHIBIT 9. EXAMPLE OF A SOURCE PLAN

<u>**Source Plan**</u>
APIs, Specialties & Intermediates (ASI)-1 Sourcing Team
March 31, 2005

To: _____   Date:_____
        Daniel Nardi, Executive Director, MMD Procurement

        _____   Date: *April 6, 2005*
        Ann Lee, Vice President, Chemical Technology & Engineering

From: *Sanjeev Majoo, Sourcing Manager, MMD Procurement*

Subject: Source Plan for *APIs, Specialties & Intermediates (ASI)-1*

Summary
Your approval is requested to authorize this Source Plan for *APIs, Specialties & Intermediates (ASI)-1*. This Source Plan/Strategy is designed to contain the ASI-1 category's future sourcing strategy and action plan (six to eighteen (18) month horizon). The figures contained herein reflect conditions at the time of the issuance of the plan. It represents a snapshot in time. It needs to be recognized that the chemicals sourcing category is highly dynamic due to the material volume demand (driven by production scheduling, inventory management and product franchise market demand) and market price volatility.

Reviewers – This document has been reviewed by:

Joseph Morrissey, Vice President, Supply Chain Management
Patricia Tway, Vice President, Regulatory & Analytical Sciences
Larry Naldi, Vice President, US Chemical Operations
Liam Murphy, Vice President, Global Chemical Quality Operations
Patrick Breen, Director, Barceloneta Technical Operations
Peter McGuigan, Laboratory Manager, Chemical Quality Operations
Francisco Martinez, Manufacturing Manager, Rahway Chemical Manufacturing
Carol Thomas, Associate Director, Regulatory & Analytical Sciences- CMC
Matt Olivier, Senior Manager, Supply Chain Management
Gavin Murdoch, Director, MMD Procurement

1

Driving Customer Centricity at Henkel[1]

It really was a stormy morning that day in early May 2008 when Kasper Rorsted, the newly appointed CEO of Henkel, called a specially arranged board meeting for later in the day. Just a few days before, he had publicly communicated his perspective on where Henkel needed to focus for the near future, as well as where he believed Henkel had the strongest potential for improvement: a true customer focus, increased strength for the global teams, and aspiring to meet the full business potential of the firm. Henkel had proclaimed the customer its top focus in 2003, but the application of this claim had yet to materialize. Part of the problem resulted from the challenges associated with Henkel's acquisition of Dial, after which Walmart demanded an intensified, global relationship from Henkel's former CEO Ulrich Lehner. The company had made substantial investments to complete the acquisition, and the massive turnover that Dial generated through Walmart moved the goal of international alignment between Henkel and its key customers to the top of the priority list. Meanwhile, the internationalization of European retailers was adding complexity to Henkel's interactions; virtually all of its key customers had expanded into new markets, mostly in Eastern Europe and Southeast Asia. These various retailers, each with their own internal processes, widened the scope of activities for which they expected Henkel to deliver excellence.

The necessary reevaluation of the strategic customer approach had just begun, but Kasper Rorsted was confident that the only way to address these pressing topics was to combine them by defining a new strategic dimension. His predecessor Ulrich Lehner had initiated a customer focus through a bottom-up direction; Rorsted believed the next step needed to be top-down. But even with this conviction, Rorsted still did not have all the implementation details at hand. To ensure company-wide clarity regarding its future perspectives, these topics had to be tackled fast.

BECOMING A GLOCAL PLAYER

It was not long ago that Lehner had taken Rorsted out to a night tour through Dusseldorf and reminded him of Henkel's history, as well as his glocal vision.

Fritz Henkel founded Henkel & Cie in Aachen on September 26, 1876, with two companions. The company was among the first European Brand Companies to undertake international operations, and regular cross-border sales began as early as 1886. By 1889, Henkel maintained a presence throughout the entire German-speaking region and the Netherlands. In the middle of the twentieth century, Konrad Henkel converted the family business, operating mainly in the German market, into a corporate group with international stature. Upon changing its legal status to a commercial partnership in 1975, Henkel comprised 70 subsidiaries and affiliated companies around the globe.

By 2008, more than 50,000 Henkel employees worked in more than 125 countries of the world. As one of the most important German branded goods company, Henkel focused on four main product categories: laundry & home care, beauty & personal care, consumer and craftsmen adhesives, and Henkel technologies. Altogether the Henkel Group generated turnover of EUR 13 million, with an earnings before interest and taxes (EBIT) of EUR 1.34 million in 2007. The bulk of its revenues and profits were realized in business-to-business contexts, where Henkel concentrated on relationships with its biggest global accounts.

Lehner also had been straightforward in recounting this history: He hoped Rorsted would continue down the road already started. Aware of where Henkel had come from and where it was going, Rorsted realized:

> *Henkel today is a glocal player, routed in Germany, but engaging in business around the globe. This approach combines our local acting and responsibility as a corporate citizen that uses holistic thinking for its global customers, while never losing touch with the values of the home base."*

A CHANGING COMPETITIVE ENVIRONMENT

Rorsted's thinking continued, especially as he remembered the recent description offered by a Henkel executive of the company's competitive picture:

> *In the fast moving consumer goods industry, retailers are becoming more powerful than the manufacturers, because they are becoming brands by themselves. As this plays out, it won't be enough to just know our business; we have to understand theirs as well. We will have to supply the big brands and own the key shelf space in the store and most important generate the most sales and profit for the store owner. Only the manufacturers that are important to the store will eventually survive.*

Since the early 2000s, the competitive environment for Henkel had continued to change drastically, in line with several major trends. To navigate them, Henkel divided its challenges into trends coming from the retailing sector and those within the manufacturing sector.

In particular, the consolidation and concentration of retailers in national markets was an EU-wide trend with vast consequences. The saturation of markets led to an increasing drive for global retailing. Then retailers entered new foreign markets at unprecedented rates, adopting leading roles in developing the newly emerging markets to ensure they were profitable. This step created potential, even as business at home was stagnating. After the initial "retail-colonization," a second wave of consolidation took place within new markets, as retailers concentrated on their own internal processes and forced suppliers, like Henkel, to adapt their local sourcing strategies. The requested global sourcing needed to harmonize IT structures, logistics, and condition systems.

A second important trend also was apparent in the retailing sector. European trade increasingly looked eastward, and the U.S. retail giant Walmart took advantage of the situation by entering the home markets of Metro, Rewe, Schlecker, and Tesco. When it appeared in the highly price sensitive German market in 1998, price pressures became even more intense for German retailers on their home front. For manufacturers like Henkel, the arrival of big retailers in markets formerly dominated by local European traders had various consequences. Walmart arrived with its own perceptions and expectations for how business should be done, which made it difficult for Henkel to apply its existing business logic, the one it had developed with European retailers.

Trade overall was growing, as a consequence of international expansion, but power shifted to the retailing side of the market. Prices were slowly approaching production costs. Margins were increasingly difficult to maintain. And the introduction of retailer brands (private labels) stressed the relationships between retailers and manufacturers even further.

HENKEL'S STRATEGY

To define the company's future, Kasper Rorsted had to acknowledge that Henkel's corporate strategy had not always focused on the customer. With a mindset focused on the product, rather than the customer, its activities followed a hybrid structure. The organizational structure combined four product categories in three divisions: (1) laundry & home care, (2) beauty & personal care, and (3) consumer and craftsmen adhesives and Henkel technologies. The divisions were cross-linked with geographic regions. Each division enjoyed a high degree of independence, and geographical regions were managed separately. However, it had changed its old mission statement—"being a specialist in applied chemistry"—to a new vision in 2003: "Henkel is a leader in brands and technologies that make people's lives easier, better and more beautiful."

Henkel's ten core values (see Figure 1 embraced a customer orientation but were not quite lived up to in practice. The first value, "we are customer driven," was of central importance for this transition. Henkel aimed to provide brands and technologies that consistently met or exceeded their customers' expectations. Since 2003, Henkel had initiated a process to align the company such that it could listen to customers, respond quickly to their needs, anticipate future needs, and provide the highest value at a fair price. The quality of Henkel's products and dialogue with customers were the means by which it sought to establish long-term partnerships, based on reliability, credibility, and mutual trust.

Through continuous organic growth of all business units around the globe and carefully selected acquisitions, the international focus of Henkel's operations grew stronger. However, it still seemed as if Henkel was pursuing a marketing-focused rather than a customer-centric strategy. Recognizing this approach, financial analysts were questioning how customer-centric the company really was. The corporate values that put the customer first appeared at odds with the applied strategy.

HENKEL'S ORGANIZATION

To pursue globalization opportunities proactively, Henkel served its global customers and business partners as they entered new markets. But Henkel was also aware that successful businesses needed a local or regional base to adapt to the widely varying needs of individual markets. For example, some countries were dominated by hypermarkets, whereas others remained nearly pure supermarket countries. Some countries were dominated by a single sales channel; others showed a high level of fragmentation. All of this variety had to be taken into consideration when designing the sales approach. Henkel needed a "glocal" approach.

Henkel's Structure

As noted previously, Henkel was structured into three divisions (see Figure 2). As a brand-driven company, Henkel focused on end consumers and often adapted to local needs.

In line with its local focus, profit and loss (P&L) responsibility laid with the local entities. Direct and independent country-level reporting lines fed into the board level, which was structured by the three business units. In each country, managers provided their local perspective, whereas the board level embraced a global perspective.

Lehner's glocal customer vision ultimately was implemented across all three business units, but the laundry and home care division was expected to take the lead in this initiative. Its goal was to realize economies of scale while simultaneously finding appealing ways to market a flagship detergent product, Persil, to a cross-regional audience. The volume of sales and the symbolic value of Persil justified Lehner's preferred course of action. Thus a cross-regional strategic business unit (SBU), tasked with marketing laundry and home care offerings on a regional basis was introduced quite early, which clearly displayed Henkel's go-to-market approach. A strategic sales unit (SSU) also was implemented, under the supervision of a Senior Corporate Vice President (CVP) for Western Europe. The main target was to define a Western European sales strategy and channel strategy, while setting guidelines for how to cooperate internationally. However, customer steering responsibility stayed in the lead country (with the exception for a few global customers like Tesco in the UK, managed out of Henkel's headquarters in Germany). Functions were bundled to serve global accounts in a coordinated manner.

These moves and cooperative teams were not externally visible though, because they provided only internal supporting functions. Many employees considered Henkel still "mainly local." But Rorsted believed in the principle that prompted the rethinking Henkel's approach to the customer and considered the laundry and home care division a good example to define further courses of action.

Henkel's Geography

From its headquarters in Düsseldorf, Germany, Henkel employed people in more than 80 countries on five continents. It also sold its products in more than 125 countries, which Henkel clustered into three main divisions: (1) Germany, EU, Africa, and the Middle East; (2) the Americas (Latin and North); and (3) Asia-Pacific. These divisions executed the corporate strategy independently but were accountable to headquarters. Furthermore, individual countries were autonomous and had their own boards. Information flowed from the bottom up to the top of the organization, independently and without any interactions. The board then provided guidelines for the three global business units, which derived their own strategies for their markets.

Europe: Decentralized Marketing of Centralized Product Capabilities.

As a glocal company Henkel tried to find the middle route to appreciate diversity, manage complexity, and still stay true to the local customer. Therefore it segmented Europe into 12 markets, such as GSA (Germany, Switzerland and Austria), the United Kingdom, France, and Spain/Portugal. Sales and marketing were locally focused. They executed the global business unit strategy. Business units in the markets and their European account managers for key retailers enjoyed some independence, but only within the boundaries of the corporate guidelines. These guidelines included a standardization scheme for branding, as well as efforts to achieve low cost production, low complexity, and quick roll-outs of best practice concepts. However, special solutions frequently were needed and "new ways invented" to overcome structural discrepancies that meant global guidelines could not perfectly meet local needs.

In terms of differentiation, Henkel wanted to be close to each customer and therefore targeted regional market penetration using flexible responses. Yet the corporate structures still did not live up to demands of facilitating such activities for major customers across international borders.

HENKEL'S CUSTOMER MANAGEMENT

Henkel served its customers' demands according to a "lead country" principle: Responsibility for managing a specific key customer laid with the country where the customer was headquartered or the country that held the highest shares of the customer's turnover. The account management team of the lead country took charge of product services, assortments, politics, and pricing. Thus, the lead country team accepted responsibility for customer-specific functions but coordinated with the other countries in which the customer and Henkel cooperated.

Increasing calls for stronger cooperation focused on the critique that there was no single key account manager for each international key account. Henkel's Düsseldorf headquarters provided generic codes of conduct and basic guidelines for logistic rules, channel strategy, allowances, customer segmenting criteria, and shelf-ready packaging, but it never engaged in operations or negotiations. These tasks were left solely to the country and the business units. Eventually, these separate business responsibilities and the lack of P&L responsibility for interactions with customers meant that a single customer interacted with various Henkel representatives, such that Henkel was missing out on synergies and losing customer satisfaction. Generic codes of conduct and a lack of direct operative engagement from top management were not viable options for customers demanding high profile services and accountability.

The historic development of internal processes for different customers suggested that these processes needed to be aligned not only internally but also with respect to channel harmonization. Further potential for growth could be found in the joint exploitation of diminishing so-called white areas, where the customer and the manufacturer were not yet present. To follow through on this potential, Rorstedt believed that Henkel had to find processes that would support cross-country and business unit cooperation.

A few notable comments stuck with Rorsted as he thought about customer management: An account manager had told him, during an informal coffee meeting, "There is so much to be done and I do not see how we can avoid upsetting our customers!"

"We are in danger of getting stuck in the middle here," a board member had warned. And as another other manager understood it, "there is really not a single competitive advantage that Henkel could defend for a long time. Henkel needs to change its mode of thinking. Otherwise, those who really understand the customers win the race!"

HENKEL'S RESPONSE

There was no knowledge transfer across business units. Several independent databases contained valuable information about key accounts and their history and preferences, but efforts to share this important information across business units, countries, or even within the same business unit were the exception rather than the rule. There were no incentives to do so, so any capitalization on internal synergies was still a distant dream. Despite the overall guidelines, the execution differed so much that it was possible for a customer to receive three different, completely independent proposals from three separate entities within Henkel for one problem. Then the customer had to choose or recombine the desired parts of each idea through a big external coordination effort. Henkel risked a situation in which the customer chose the best solution and simply wanted it applied across all its divisions. Without transparency of actions or consistent solutions for the customer, it could not resolve these issues.

In addition, structural differences in Henkel's business units and varied decision-making processes prevented Henkel from adopting one strategy per customer. In response, it incorporated international key account management (IKAM) as a coordinative unit within each business unit to frame the relationship for the customer. The key hypothesis for leveraging key account management internationally was that only a comprehensive alignment of both Henkel and its customers globally would lead to acceptance of all Henkel's initiatives, which in turn would ensure better performance by both partners in the markets.

Overall, Henkel's response to customers' needs thus could be described as a chain of individual initiatives, instead of one leading program that combined global guidelines with local demands. Despite its awareness of customers' demands, Henkel was still struggling with this combination and the goal of showing only "one face to the customer." The efforts already undertaken needed to be coordinated and put into an overarching framework.

ROLES, SKILLS, AND DEVELOPMENT OF IKAM

Implementing successful customer management was not like any other challenge Rorsted and the board had previously faced. They were conscious that the social qualities were just as important as professional capabilities for relationship development, so these were the top priorities for internal training to eventually move the IKAM system even to global account management (GAM).

First, understanding of the role of account management had to be changed. The company-wide perception viewed IKAMs as simple representatives of the supplier or salespeople, rather than as solution providers. Henkel also needed to communicate its new focus on human resources, to emphasize the line manager as the ultimate manager who ensured proper training and personnel development to enable employees to excel.

Second, from an interpersonal skills perspective, it was crucial for the IKAMs to identify with the customer. Account representatives could only serve their customers effectively and to their satisfaction if they understood their motivation and goals. It would not be enough to adopt a coordinative role. Henkel had to show true leadership in developing relationships on personal and professional fronts to be accepted as a solution provider. The market was full of account managers who merely reacted to customers' demands instead of anticipating them and developing joint solutions.

When building a team with members from both sides, Henkel frequently encountered the problem of "falling lines"—the employees from each were similar in their personal traits (e.g., gender, nationality, experience) and had connections on various levels, but they lacked such relations with members of the other party. The solution seemed to be heterogeneous teams that could cross-fertilize each other's ideas and truly leverage their diversity. The global perspective for the forthcoming GAM thus would take shape.

Third, regarding professional capabilities, many tools used by different departments were not fully understood by the prospective GAM. They previously did not have to worry about future account planning or forecasting of sales figures. Asking for an integrative perspective that combined knowledge from different business units with profound knowledge of the customer's markets was as difficult as getting an understanding of the customer's business.

Beyond a cross-divisional understanding of the customer's business, the assessment needed to go in two directions: top-down and bottom-down. Two key performance indicators (KPIs) thus were essential: turnover and direct account profitability. The prospective GAM needed to define an overarching strategy; regional and local KAMs then had to turn these premises into concrete actions that would enable them to meet the bottom line each year. Finally, everyone had to understand that successful sales operations were first and foremost a team effort.

Hence, a substantial lack of professional experience as IKAM could easily result in quick satisfaction in areas that presented huge possibilities for improvements once looked at in depth. It also was very difficult to determine and then communicate what methods were not succeeding, because the effort topic was new to everybody.

MAKING THE CASE...

Rorsted headed to the meeting room, thinking, "In tough times with tough customers, we have to have a tough strategy. And by all means, we are a world of customers—our 2007 annual motto."

Whereas IKAM had been a starting point for Henkel to engage in value-added services, it needed to be much more. The IKAMs had to be groomed to become true GAMs, respected advisors to their customers. Henkel would run the risk, sooner or later, of losing momentum with its global customers if it could not deliver a program that operated across all divisions, driven by top management, to provide good answers for each strategic customer on a global basis. With all these thoughts in mind, Rorsted pulled open the door to start the board meeting.

ENDNOTES

1   Prepared by Lisa Napolitano, Nicole Rosenkranz, and Matthias Tietz under Christoph Senn's supervision. Franz Speer, Director International Key Account Management, provided significant assistance.

FIGURE 1. HENKEL'S 10 CORE VALUES

We are customer driven.

We develop superior brands and technologies.

We aspire to excellence in quality.

We strive for innovation.

We embrace change.

We are successful because of our people.

We are committed to shareholder value.

We are dedicated to sustainability and corporate social responsibility.

We communicate openly and actively.

We preserve the tradition of an open family company.

Source: Henkel webpage 2008: *www.henkel.com*.

FIGURE 2. HENKEL'S COMPANY STRUCTURE

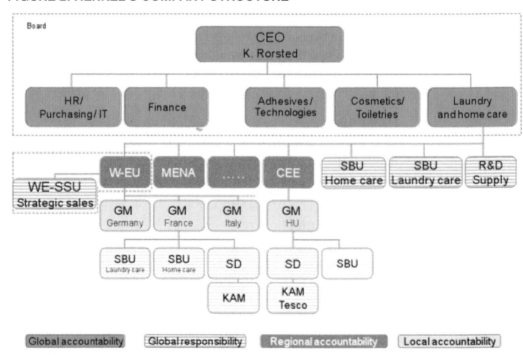

Source: Henkel Presentation, HR Department (2007).

Global Customer Solutions at DHL[1]

The abrupt landing of the plane sent a gush of adrenaline through Dirk Gardner's veins—and he was already on the tips of his toes. He was hastily making his way to DHL headquarters after his boss had called him earlier in the day. There was to be a meeting with the DHL Global Commercial Board to discuss the challenges of selling "integrated solutions," the next step in the evolution of the company's Global Account Management (GAM) program. Gardner had enjoyed a lot of success setting up the account management programs at DHL, especially considering the changing landscape that arose as DHL had acquired different companies. But this meeting might have a major impact, not only on his own career but on the company's overall ability to continue as a trusted leader for its major clients. Customers were demanding that providers integrate their capabilities to create more value. And as Gardner had explained over and over to senior management, single product offerings, such as express shipping, were being commoditized when sold as stand-alone products. Integrated solutions had to succeed; otherwise, the strategy underlying DHL's acquisition quest would be at risk.

THE BEGINNING

DHL (named for its founders: Dalsey, Hillblom, and Lynn) started out as a document courier in 1969, laying the foundation for an entirely new industry. The next few years saw the company expand throughout the Americas, the Asia Pacific region, and Europe. In 2002, eight years after Gardner joined DHL, it was acquired by Deutsche Post (DPWN), which then went on to acquire more than 100 companies, including the largest freight forwarder (Danzas-AEI), the leading European road freight company, and the leading domestic parcel companies in the United Kingdom, France, Spain, and Benelux. By 2005, Gardner was one of 285,000 DHL employees who generated roughly $65 billion in annual sales.

He had been with the company for 14 years, so he well knew that DHL's GAM program represented its answer to increasing competitive pressures, not only on DHL but for its major clients. On the micro-level, the implementation had been primarily customer driven, because large customers demanded at least a regional and usually a global approach to doing business with DHL. From the customers' perspective, it was logical to leverage their buying power and request globally harmonized solutions for a business that dealt primarily with cross-border transactions and services. Initially, the most common requirements from the customer side were consistent services worldwide, comprehensive contracts with selected suppliers, following the ideal of "one-stop shopping," and a competitive price. On a macro-level the program was a necessary next step for DHL, following such trends as globalization and industry consolidation. Technological advancements and increasing outsourcing, as much as off-shoring activities, focused attention on efficient supply chain management and logistic services.

When the first 27 global accounts were identified in 1995, the GAMs that served them were all based in the country where the customer's headquarters was located, following a lead country principle. For that reason, they formed part of DHL's country organization and reported to the country manager. But at that point in time, GAMs sold only a single product: Air Express. This loose setup creates some special challenges, because the account managers seemed just to create extra requests, additional reports, and more expenditures for the country's cost center. As one manager complained,

> *Nobody really understood what we were doing and how we could possibly contribute to better numbers for the country profit & loss. I think it was really difficult for our country Managing Directors (MDs) to see the advantages of the program directly after its implementation."*

Still, those individually managed accounts ultimately reached combined annual revenues of almost 200 million Euros. In 1997, Gardner's boss had identified him as one of the most experienced GAMs and asked him to take the lead in reorganizing the global accounts. His target: Generate revenues of 500 million Euros by the pool of 20 global accounts. Revisiting this early stage of GAM program development in his mind, Gardner thought:

> *Good that we implemented a 'needs based segmentation' to come up with some industry wide solution sets, otherwise we would still be in the stone age of Air Express Service.*

In 2000, following extensive consultation with DHL's regional and country organizations, Gardner and his colleagues undertook a major upgrade to the existing informal setup. They created a new Global Customer Logistics (GCL) organization, outside the business units. Because it built on existing ideas, the updated program was not perceived as something completely new. Nor was it unilaterally imposed, which enabled DHL members to realize that the improvements were necessary to meet the evolving needs of global customers. Gardner and his team created vertical industry hierarchies, headed by an industry director, and transferred the reporting and costs of the GAMs to a central budget. Thus they encouraged knowledge sharing among GAMs. At the request of the regions, the GCL also had a "shadow" profit & loss account, which helped ensure financial alignment with the group's objectives.

In 2003, the next major revision of the GAM program resulted from a rebranding effort for all business units, under a new DHL umbrella brand. The 100 companies that DPWN had acquired were all rebranded as part of DHL and a new organization, Global Customer Solutions (GCS), formed, covering DHL's four main units: DHL Express, DHL (road) Freight, DHL Contract Logistics, and DHL Air/Ocean forwarding. In addition to continuing to serve as the GAM for a key customer, Gardner led the design of the new organization, which required integrating the programs employed by all the DHL business units for the first time. After the integration, Express no longer dominated in terms of revenue generation.

There were both challenges and good reasoning associated with these new changes. Gardner reminded himself of just how challenging the project had been—far more than he had expected. The other business units lacked experience managing a formal GAM program. His first mistake had been to assume that they would be supportive. But in the end, his arguments had prevailed, for several reasons that he could summarize:

First of all, more and more customers were demanding a global approach across all the businesses. DHL could not afford to have a GAM program for express but not for the other BUs. The nature of our clients' business changed from local to global, so we had no choice but to grow with them.

Secondly, our customers supply chains were becoming more complicated, integrating capabilities to form a holistic solution that required global coordination. With the exception of Express, no such organization existed.

Third, DHL had witnessed a distinct trend amongst our major accounts toward reducing the number of suppliers and leveraging their buying power. Thus, working more closely with them made sure we were still the preferred business partner across all the business units.

Despite these strong arguments, it had been a tough sell to the business unit heads to convince them of the changing needs of our customers.

To ensure that the arguments translated into reality and achieve the buy-in of all the business units, the new GCS appointed a managing director at the highest executive management level, directly connected to the board members. Therefore, GAMs would report to the highest level in the organization and could attain the formal authority needed to implement the GAM strategies and motivate others in the company. When in 2006 DHL's parent company acquired a huge contract logistics company, Exel plc, Gardner and his colleagues had to redefine their global accounts again, to integrate these new global customers (see Figure 1, Appendix)..

Considering his contributions, DHL senior management greatly respected Gardner, as well as the role GCS had for developing business with global customers. Cross-selling had improved, giving the GAMs much more status and respect among the business units, beyond just buying power. Furthermore, the GAMs' ability to interact with various interest groups simultaneously and actively maintain relationships across business units, internally and externally, made them valued co-workers. However, even within these greatly improved structures, it was clear that overall success depended tremendously on the capabilities of the individual GAMs. Their skills would always be necessary to maximize positive impacts on the organization. The recently shifted governance for the GCS also reflected its importance; the CEO of GCS now reported directly to the CEO of Deutsche DHL, a strong indicator of the substantial attention the GCS and GAMs received. By now, revenues for GCS exceeded 8 billion Euro—a notable increase for a group that had begun only 13 years earlier (see Figures 2 – 5, Appendix).

Gardner was motivated to maintain this level of success by delivering a compelling report about how DHL could leverage the lessons learned through the development of its lead customer, Stamford Ltd. in the GCS program. Their relationship—Stamford was a major player in the computer hardware industry, and DHL was their preferred supplier of supply chain and freight services—was worth analyzing in detail. Both parties enjoyed a high level of understanding; DHL's involvement in Stamford, under Gardner's leadership, was so extensive that it understood the client's business and long-term strategic goals in detail—at times, Gardner could even surprise Stamford's management.

PREPARING FOR THE MEETING

To prevent any surprises on his side, Dirk Gardner went over the agenda for the meeting once more in the cab. His task today was to bring the Global Commercial Board Members up to speed on the lessons learned from the most recent developments with Stamford Ltd.

As Stamford's GAM, Gardner was responsible for creating integrated, global supply chain solutions; he hoped to distill the abstract outcomes of this best practice example to describe actual managerial practices for the board. Although DHL had sold many integrated solutions, Stamford had presented real challenges for developing a solution that could be supported by all of DHL's business units. If this complex solution and the methods to reach it could be summarized as general best practices, it might provide a powerful catalyst for DHL to move to the next level of internal integration, as well as offer a powerful engine for growth. If DHL could develop the necessary systematic components and train employees to work with great passion, this example would lead to a wide array of applications that would ensure DHL's top position for years to come.

Gardner decided to start his presentation by outlining the competitive landscape, then detail the cornerstones of Stamford's requests. Next, he would highlight the core challenges for this project, focusing first on the internal perspective and then on external demands. He needed to give the board a succinct idea of the solutions, because even though they were highly specific to Stamford, the issues he had to resolve were generic, in terms of solving challenges when selling integrated supply chain solutions. Finally, he would outline the key lessons and recommendations for next steps, which he hoped the board would endorse. Gardner believed this structure for his presentation was the best way to help the board recognize the critical challenge DHL was facing: how to translate best practices into a general business model.

COMPETITIVE LANDSCAPE

When Asia outpaced Europe as the main center for IT and computer-related manufacturing, the boom for Asian economies demanded a restructuring by the world's major freight carriers. Historically, there had been two alternatives to ship products from Asia to Europe: Use a freight forwarder to ship bulk items to a European warehouse for subsequent distribution, or rely on a more expensive, faster express solution provided by an integrator such as DHL or UPS. However, experience showed that the integrators struggled to handle shipment volumes efficiently. Freight forwarders were hampered by slow transit time and little ability to track shipments; they rarely provided "the last mile" service either, by moving products from distribution centers to their final destinations. The high pressure goal was to combine the capabilities of both services into a single product that offered shorter transit times, greater visibility, and reasonable prices.

DHL's overall strategic intent had long been to provide the widest array of services under one brand, which drove its acquisition of so many transport and logistic provider companies. Executive management believed that this broad portfolio of services would be key to creating a competitive advantage to attract companies such as Stamford. They were proven correct; soon, Stamford Ltd. asked all major freight carriers to pitch for a "one-stop shopping" concept to handle its entire distribution system.

STAMFORD LTD.

Stamford asked DHL specifically to develop a groundbreaking supply chain solution for direct delivery of products from its Asian contract manufacturer to individual dealerships in Europe. Stamford wanted full end-to-end visibility, weekly end-to-end performance, and a single invoice with a flat rate per package (after successful delivery to the final destination). It also wanted onerous liabilities moved to DHL for cases of parcel loss, independent of where and how the loss took place.

DHL had a long history of successful cooperation with Stamford, in which they consistently found ways to achieve their mutual goals of providing end consumers with the best products, quickly and conveniently. The demand for an integrated, faster, cheaper solution across the entire delivery chain represented by far the biggest challenge to date though. From the beginning, any solution would need to involve all four business units (BUs) at DHL simultaneously.

INTERNAL CHALLENGES

By responding to the changing world of logistics and Stamford's high demands with an integrated supply chain solution program, DHL was a step ahead of its competition. But some fundamental internal shortcomings seemed tough to overcome at the beginning of the project:

Sitting down with the [business units] for a first brainstorming session on how to best approach Stamford's demands already revealed a lot of internal room for improvement. It was clear that the solution would have to be presented as a "DHL" solution rather than a solution by a particular business unit or a particular DHL region The business unit stakeholders were all concerned about how to protect their profit and loss sheets.

Lack of commitment

People had very different ideas about the success chances of such a supply chain solution. The idea that GCS would provide a new perspective on how to address issues was not entirely new, but most of the team actually questioned the need for change. Stamford was pushing for the program, but many managers inside DHL were unsure, whether and how this supply chain solution would ever work in practice.

They were concerned about the feasibility of the project, which seemed to threaten their business units' future revenue streams. When DHL managers from Europe and Asia first became involved, it thus was a challenge for Gardner and his team of GAMs to unite everybody behind common goals. During initial talks about necessary delivery times between distribution centers, one European colleague perceptively realized that Asian managers would hesitate to commit to such an estimate, because if they made a mistake, "They could not possibly confront their boss with this without losing face." Consequently, the Asian managers would argue for a misunderstanding of the proposed agreements, withdrawing from their earlier statements.

Most of the revenue derived from the solution would go to the forwarding division, which would be responsible for the transport leg from Asia to Europe. However, the Express and Freight lines, as the second and third largest business units, were unwilling to commit to any agreement that did not assure their revenues. They were concerned that their unit's internal margins would be sacrificed to allow Airfreight (the biggest unit) to offer better deals on its bulk business. Thus the entire venture was in jeopardy because of internal reluctance to commit to the project—which largely reflected the managers' disbelief in their own capabilities.

Chargeable weight and internal pricing

Gardner's team also experienced obstacles related to the calculation for chargeable weight, the basis for pricing a service in the transportation business. Just before the project kick-off, this issue had reached a crisis point. The differences were substantial, especially between air and land freight: Airfreight applied a higher factor to its air volume calculation. But the client demanded one end-to-end price, so it was out of the question to featured multiple chargeable weights on the bill.

A special meeting was called to resolve these DHL-specific issues. The emphasis was on getting prices settled at the business unit level, notwithstanding the different pricing approaches. Although DHL needed different chargeable weights to calculate its revenues and internal pricing, these values were much less interesting to the client. By taking the client's perspective, DHL ultimately derived a solution: report a carefully calculated weighted average of the chargeable weights to the client, even as internally, billing by each business unit would continue with the existing chargeable weight terms. This resolution only applied to one element of the pricing strategy though. Considering the request for a single flat rate, the winning strategy eventually was to calculate the price backward. Participants agreed on a competitive flat rate per unit of chargeable weight. Then all business units claimed their share, each agreeing on a certain discount for the overall benefit of winning the contract. This discount required freight, as the incumbent, to shoulder the additional costs for overall coordination of shipments and billing. Although the business units all left the table with slightly lower revenues, they also enjoyed lower costs. Internally, a contractual agreement guaranteed stable revenues, calculable for all units. In setting up this contract, Dirk Gardner had to orchestrate and control all the various interests of the business units in a way that allowed them to benefit proportionally from their own input and commitment. From the "driver's seat" as the controlling GAM, he received the full support of his CEO, because "Gardner knew he could not compel the business units to accept a deal without the blessing from above."

End-to-end visibility

On the second week of the project's dry run, just after resolving the difficult internal revenue distribution challenge, some new issues arose on the cost side. Stamford was demanding end-to-end visibility at all times during the process, but a tool that would create a platform where Stamford's managers could log on and track their packages simply did not exist. Each business unit had a separate system to track its packages, and the software marketplace did not offer a single system that could facilitate monitoring across the entire business.

Some participants suggested developing a new in-house system to solve the problem, but the massive costs of such an undertaking froze that idea. None of the business units was willing to take on these costs; instead, they each touted the benefits of their system, which would prevent them from having to change. The final compromise—which was also the lowest cost solution and easiest to implement—used an existing tracking system by freight that was already in operation for Stamford's products. Some enhancement was necessary to include the smaller business units and transcontinental flights.

EXTERNAL CHALLENGES

Exchange rate risks

Even after they dealt with the internal DHL concerns, the team around Dirk Gardner could not relax; external challenges waited. Multiple currencies that were involved in the deal, but Stamford wanted to be billed only once, using only one currency. DHL therefore needed to construct a system to convert foreign exchange rates across business units and determine which currency would be most suitable for the final invoice. The internal agreements were based on and designed around stable revenues for all participants, so they had to find a stable currency that would not swing up and down their revenues like a rollercoaster.

A dedicated GCS project team member had built a complex model that could divide the revenue stream according to the different currencies involved, independent of the precise route that the parcel would travel. The model showed that U.S. dollars, in most cases, was the most used currency. Its close link with the Hong Kong dollar and the Singapore dollar also suggested there would be less volatility in these exchange rates.

Later in the project, these models of the development of the exchange rate also revealed different scenarios that would result from the development of the U.S. dollar against the Euro or British pound. Gardner and his team also hedged the risk of exchange rates by creating bands within which the dollar would be calculated at a certain exchange rate, reassessed only if it was out of those bounds. If this bandwidth were exceeded, a different exchange rate would apply for the subsequent band. Thus the risk was shared equally by the contracting parties.

Liabilities

Gardner hated admitting that every now and then a package would be broken or get lost, but it was an inherent part of the shipping business. In this situation though, the liabilities for lost packages were not clear to either contract partner. Previous discussions had revolved around the two standards for settling a claim: Under the Warsaw Convention, a claim could result in reimbursements of US$20 per lost kilogram of freight. With the French CMA standard, reimbursement was only US$7 per kilogram. Normally, cargo lost "in the air" would be handled according to the Warsaw Convention, whereas packages lost "on land" would fall under the CMA. Stamford wanted coverage under the Warsaw Convention for the entire transportation. Although it was a significant concern for the freight business unit, eventually Gardner was able to persuade it to accept this additional liability.

Reporting performance

After discussions on the managerial level, Stamford stressed its wish for performance evaluations and methods to identify improvement potential. It asked for a single document, provided on a weekly basis, that would summarize all shipments made during the previous week and the time needed for their accomplishment. Because they were reluctant to report on anything other than their individual performance, the business units resisted being held responsible for the entire delivery service.

Again, it took more than just personal methods of persuasion to wrest control and responsibility from the business units. By skillfully weighing responsibility and workload against revenue streams, Gardner encouraged the centralization of performance reporting. He also stressed that "working for the same company, all units in the end had to unite in the effort of delivering the best results as a team, so why not start measuring them on that?"

But buy-in was not guaranteed. Gardner had to take action regarding the reporting decision; he agreed to accept extra responsibility, for the greater good of controlling the performance reports from a centralized GAM perspective. With this approach, new performance charts were created to measure overarching performance. In contrast with the old system, business units no longer needed to fill out their own performance control charts. As Gardner told his colleagues,

> the more decisions, responsibility and cost you take away from them, the happier the business units will eventually be, because then they can concentrate on the business. But that also helps us in centralizing the responsibilities with GCS.

The control tower operated by the U.K. freight arm handled most coordination of shipments, so Gardner decided that it should also gather the reporting information on the few other lags, as a supervising unit.

Single point of contact

Finally, Gardner's team had to find a way to bundle communication with the client and provide a single point of contact that would communicate all the gathered data and handle all client requests. This design had immense internal implications for the power distribution too, which made it perhaps the most challenging tasks. Before the project could begin, the client demanded that "A single individual person functions centrally within DHL as the decision taker and handles all client requests from a compromising and integrative point of view." Therefore, the leading GAM would be responsible for managing and executing the entire contract. In Gardner's interpretation, it meant

> taking an authoritative function above the business unit level that would add additional value above the sum of values the units provided. To add all the extra value demanded, it was crucial to also accept more responsibility as a GAM, clearly leaving behind only the coordinating function."

The new position also came with the responsibility of making decisions that none of the business units could make alone, much less afford. It was the GAM's vital role to guide the entire team of people, representing different business units, to achieve more together than they would individually. Externally, the GAM would be the only person Stamford needed to address with questions about the contract. But business units were used to communicating with the client directly, so they were at first unwilling to give away their contacts and control.

To meet the client's request without upsetting the business units, Gardner personally took over this position as a neutral person to communicate with the client. The business units did not like giving up their direction contacts to the GCS, but he believed this channel needed a strong character who was experienced with adversity. The move was bound to be controversial, because Gardner, without touching the units' revenues, was challenging their control. His position lessened their power to make critical decisions, but because he was able to defend them with sound arguments, the business units eventually would learn to like it. Gardner also had worked hard to maintain good personal relationships with his colleagues, so the units had good reason to trust him.

SOFT DEMANDS ON GAMS

Gardner's boss honored him and his team on the first anniversary of the project:

> *Any GAM who takes the lead for such a project has an incredible amount of responsibility. We need to work towards the status where every GAM feels they have a mission to fulfill, something greater to take care of than just their own job. Then we will continue to celebrate anniversaries like this one.*

Gardner knew his boss was correct: He had experienced the imperfect settings, the unclear structures, the undefined responsibilities, and even the lack of belief in his own capabilities. It would have been easier to give up, but instead he had coped with them, showing great strength of character.

As a leading GAM at DHL, Gardner also felt that he was being entrusted with massive responsibilities. It was not only his job, his income, and his family that he felt responsible for; he also considered his colleagues. Thinking along these lines truly motivated him; without this mindset and values, he would never have been able to develop a "can-do" attitude in the face of all the adversity he had faced.

This was what they were celebrating. The entire organization gained an understanding of its own capabilities, such that employees believed in themselves and the company as a whole. Getting this project up and running created a great mood in the workplace, with employees willing to acknowledge imperfections and try to improve, instead of just complaining that nothing would change. Members of the team also had learned to accept losses while remaining focused, without getting caught up in the details. Gardner felt that he had inspired his colleagues with his personal desire to get things done. Maybe he even showed them how a higher level of understanding overcomes a segmented, unit-level way of thinking and offers an overview of all business units as one company. Gardner did want to rest on his laurels though, because

> *It was crucial to maintain the drive and perspective; after all, this was only the start. That it had worked once was great, but only if we can filter out the critical learnings from our experience and distill them into more abstract terms on a higher company-wide level are we able to repeat the same success story with another client soon.*

This drive was exactly what the board wanted, by understanding the possibilities for a company-wide rollout of the lessons learned from the Stamford case. Gardner was prepared to put all his motivation from his success story into his presentation to the board.

THE DHL GLOBAL COMMERCIAL BOARD MEETING

In the meeting room, the chill of the air conditioning was too cold for Gardner's liking. But maybe it would help him stay cool during his discussion with the board. The DHL Global Board consisted of global commercial heads for each of the DHL Business units (Express, Freight, Contract Logistics and Forwarding) and was chaired by the GCS managing director. Its broad mandate was to set commercial strategy and priorities for the DHL Group. The GCS managing director served as the chair because he could be neutral across business units and also effectively articulate the future needs of DHL's largest, most important customers.

All the board members had come to understand and accept the value of GCS; nevertheless, debate continued within DHL regarding to how best to take GCS forward and to address the remaining integration challenges. Each board member represented the interests of a single business unit, so even as they realized the need for further changes, they considered the practical difficulties of implementing these changes.

For example, the senior vice president of the forwarding unit had started his career with Danzas, whose business model had focused on airport-to-airport forwarding and subcontracted collection and delivery to third parties. It prided itself on its flexibility to create tailored solutions to meet each customer's requirements; this vice president had been the most reluctant to support GCS.

The senior vice president representing the contract logistics business had worked for Exel for many years, focusing on "4 walls" activity. Forwarding activity had not been very important, and that company subcontracted out many services. Its targeted customer solutions had tended to be profitable and national, focused on retail and consumer customers. The request for complex global solutions seemed very risky to this board member.

Similar to Gardner, the Express head had been with DHL for years. He remembered when DHL Express had "controlled" the customer's entire supply chain. Because Express was an asset-based business with a lot of infrastructure and planes to finance, this vice president believed that control of the solution was the key to keeping these assets well utilized.

The head of the Road Freight business had a slightly different perspective: He regarded DHL's business as a commodity with small margins. Keeping things simple was important, which included avoiding IT and other costs. Unlike his colleagues, he knew that the Freight business unit could not aspire to control the supply chain.

These were the board members Gardner had to convince of the need for change. He knew his boss would support him, provided his arguments were well made. But his boss, as the chair, also needed to steer a balanced course to reach any decision and ensure consensus on any outcomes. Thus his boss introduced the next subject on the board's agenda:

> *I have asked Dirk to make a short presentation to us on the Stamford solution we implemented last year. As you know this was one of DHL's first truly integrated solutions and I thought it*

would be useful to understand the challenges Dirk has had in implementing this with Stamford. We also need to understand how we can make this process easier in the future and I have asked Dirk to include a list of recommendations which we should consider implementing to help us drive our business forward more effectively.

Gardner reminded himself to focus on the overall scope of his presentation as he stood up to address his audience.

ENDNOTES

1   Prepared by Lisa Napolitano, Nicole Rosenkranz, and Matthias Tietz under Christoph Senn's supervision. Tim Harford, Managing Director GCS Express Business Development, provided significant assistance.

FIGURE 1. A GLOBAL PLAYER WITH STRONG DIVISIONS

Deutsche Post ✖ World Net			
MAIL	EXPRESS	LOGISTICS	FINANCIAL SERVICES
Deutsche Post ✖	DHL	DHL	Postbank
Worldwide	Worldwide	Worldwide	Germany
• DHL Global Mail – biggest network for mail distribution worldwide • Delivers mail to about 40 million households in Germany • More than 71 million shipments a day	• No. 1 in cross border express • Strong presence in 220+ countries and territories • More than 4.2 million customers worldwide • 120,000 destinations	• No. 1 in global contract logistics • No. 1 in global air freight • No. 1 in global ocean freight • 3,000 locations • Strong customer base (50% of Forbes 500 companies)	• Germany's leading retail bank • 12.3 million customers • 17.2 million savings accounts USA • Worldwide finance services for logistics industry

Source: DHL Corporate Information

Notes: In 2006, revenues were 63 billion, earnings 3.9 billion, and DHL had approximately 500,000 employees.

FIGURE 2. WHAT ARE DHL GLOBAL CUSTOMER SOLUTIONS?

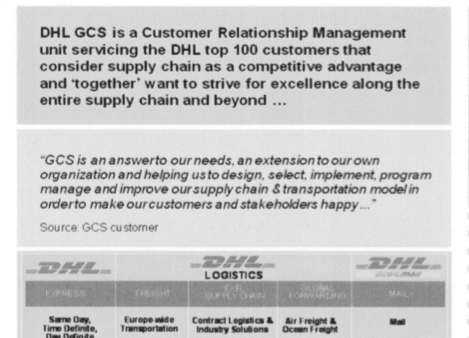

Source: DHL Corporate Information

FIGURE 3. GLOBAL CUSTOMER ACCOUNT TEAMS

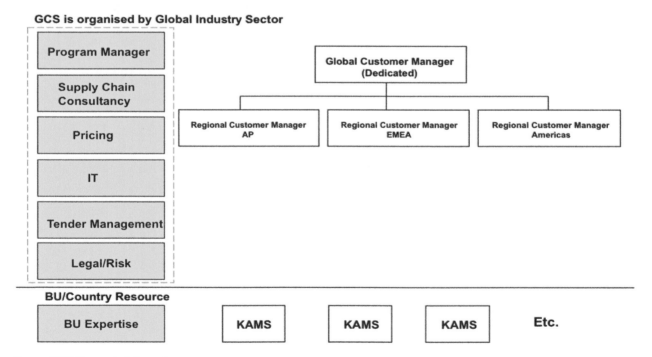

Source: DHL Corporate Information

FIGURE 4. CUSTOMER SEGMENTATION AT DHL

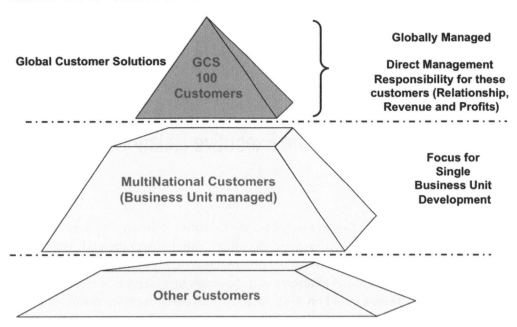

Source: DHL Corporate Information

FIGURE 5. GCS OBJECTIVES: DRIVEN BY THE OVERALL DHL VISION

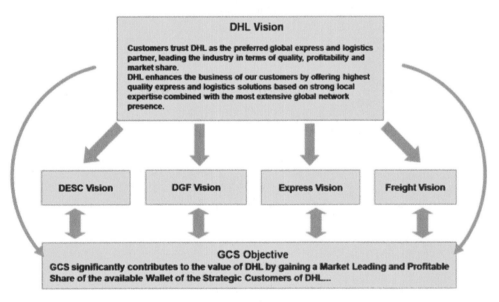

Source: DHL Corporate Information

Siemens: The Executive Relations Program[1]

In 2009, Siemens instituted the Executive Relations Program (ERP) at the corporate level. The ERP matched Siemens' executive committee members with major customers. Preliminary results suggested that the program was highly effective in improving revenues via optimizing Siemens' relationships with key customers. The 10 members of Siemens' senior leadership team focused on 99 key accounts; all executive team members participated in the program. CEO Peter Löscher was executive sponsor for eleven key customers; the most committed executive was responsible for more than 15 customers. As the program evolved and more customers were added, the Account Management Program Office (AMPO) was wondering if the ERP's success could eventually become a problem. Executive committee commitment had been great and members were dedicating significant time and effort to "their" customers; but they also had 'day jobs.' AMPO staff wondered if 99 customerss was the appropriate number for the program. Should there be more? Or should there be less?

THE EXECUTIVE RELATIONSHIP PROGRAM

Peter Löscher had been Siemens' chief executive for nearly five years; he had good reasons for being enthusiastic. As he told the full executive committee:

> *"Today is a very special day. You all have done a terrific job! Paulo just walked me through the full-year report on our executive relations program: Revenues from our KAM driven customers have grown at more than twice the rate of our overall customer base — that's what I call a great success."*

Löscher was referring to Paulo Martinez,[2] Corporate Vice President at Siemens; Martinez headed the Corporate Development Department in charge of Key Account Management. Martinez and his SVP for Key Account Management and Market Development, Mats Goetze, had been instrumental in initiating the program that personally involved all executive committee members in Siemens' relationships with its most important customers. Executive committee member, Robert Traber, was very pleased to hear the news:

> *"Well, that's what I have always said: It is great when we personally engage with our large customers. That is how we make our personal network available to Siemens, grow it and get direct touch to our most important customers. Additionally, we support our Key Account Managers (KAMs) by making visible that we want to be informed how things proceed. This is the way executive relationship can help KAMs achieve their customer-specific goals.*

Actually, last night I met that guy from Krienrath Systems. They have been championing the production industry and are planning to invest heavily in several Asian countries where we will see tremendous future growth. I have just asked Manuela, who manages this account, to prepare a detailed proposal for them."

"So why don't you talk to Paulo?" Löscher replied, *"Maybe Krienrath Systems should be included as part of the Executive Relationship Program. You seem to know them quite well already, so you may be in a good position to be their executive sponsor."* Traber considered this a great idea and invited Paulo for a meeting the next day.

Siemens AG — 1847 to 2012

Siemens had a storied history. Founded by electrical engineering pioneer Werner von Siemens in 1847 in a small workshop in Berlin, Siemens initially worked to commercialize von Siemens' ideas for an improved electric telegraph system.[3] The new company won the contract to build Europe's long-distance telegraph line, and quickly expanded into many European countries. By 1870, Siemens had laid the first telegraph connection between London and Calcutta (Kolkata), India. Siemens would go on to build the world's first electric elevator and install the first electric street lighting. During the next century, through continued innovation in electrical engineering, acquisitions, and partnerships, Siemens would grow to become one of Germany's and the world's largest and most successful industrial corporations. By the late 1970s, Siemens had replaced Westinghouse as the world's number two electrical engineering and manufacturing company, after General Electric (U.S.), whose history and portfolio were quite similar to those of Siemens.

Notwithstanding Siemens' remarkable success, two major trends caused the firm to question its engineering- and acquisition-driven- conglomerate structure. In the 1980s and 1990s, despite major R&D investments, Siemens was not as quick as smaller Silicon Valley companies in innovating. Further, Siemens had difficulties competing effectively with lower-cost Japanese manufacturers in the fast-evolving semiconductor and computing industries.[4] Simultaneously, growth slowed in Siemens' traditional European markets — still three-quarters of total revenues. By the end of the century, Siemens began a radical program of restructuring and cultural change. Siemens sold underperforming units that could not achieve profitable market leadership, including Infineon (semiconductor division). Across Siemens units, managers had greater accountability for profitable growth, and Siemens placed increasing emphasis on opportunities in Asia and the Americas.

By 2002, Siemens' business portfolio spanned wired and wireless communications; industrial automation logistics; building infrastructure; lighting; power generation, transmission and distribution; transportation and automotive systems; and medical solutions. In spite of pressure to further focus this diverse organization, management believed that Siemens' units held significant opportunities for synergies that created differential advantage.

During the 2000s, Siemens continued its transition to a market-oriented company. In 2005, the company introduced a new corporate vision that provided a focal point for Siemens going forward: The concept of *global megatrends* driving customer markets. Four key themes would define Siemens future product and service offerings: *Changing demographics*, *urbanization*, *climate change*, and *globalization* (Exhibit 1). Siemens' R&D and sales and marketing efforts would focus on vertical markets that these trends impacted. After joining Siemens as

President and CEO in July 2007, Peter Löscher supplemented these megatrends with a new *guiding principle* around which Siemens' vision could be communicated — *sustainability*.

The new strategic vision empowered Siemens' drive to rationalize and simplify its business portfolio. By October 2011, Siemens operated in four consolidated sectors — *Industry, Energy, Healthcare*, and the newly created *Infrastructure & Cities* — directly responsive to the urbanization megatrend; each sector comprised several divisions. Exhibit 2 shows Siemens operating structure in early 2012. Internal real estate, information technology, and financial services groups supported Siemens' business portfolio. Siemens also retained significant equity stakes in several joint ventures like Nokia Siemens Networks (50/50 joint venture with Nokia in telecommunications infrastructure). Exhibit 3 shows current key performance indicators and revenue split by region. Exhibit 4 depicts executive committee members and their responsibilities.

As fiscal 2011 drew to a close, Siemens reported record operating results: Revenue increased by seven percent to €73.5 billion. Income from continuing operations was €7.0 billion, a 65 percent increase over fiscal 2010.[5] Siemens continued its strategy of regional diversification and employed 360,000 people across the globe.[6] Peter Löscher stated:

> *"With a strong fourth quarter in a turbulent economic environment, we ended fiscal 2011 with record operating results. With our new four Sectors organization, we have aligned our business even more closely with our customers. Siemens has a strong portfolio and stands for stability and confidence in troubled times. We are well positioned for […] surpassing the €100 billion revenue threshold in the medium term."* [7]

Siemens' Objectives: Today and Tomorrow

Siemens defined three strategic directions for continuing on its path of sustainable value creation and excellence[8]:

- **Innovation: Focus on innovation-driven growth markets.** So-called 'green' revenues had grown dramatically. Siemens environmental portfolio, comprising products and solutions that contributed directly to environmental protection and climate change mitigation, already represented over 40 percent of total revenues — €29.9 billion. These revenues were expected to rise to €40 billion within three years.

    In 2010, Siemens' *environmental portfolio* helped customers save a record 317 million tons CO_2, roughly equal to one percent of global CO_2 emissions. Products comprised technologies for renewable energies (wind, solar, and thermal); environmental technologies (water, and air pollution control); plus products and solutions with exceptional energy efficiency like combined-cycle power plants, traffic management, and efficient lightning.

Whereas traditional thinking often assumed a conflict between economically efficient and environmentally friendly solutions, Siemens — and its customers — often found that environmentally friendly solutions were more economical.

- **Customers: Get closer to customers.** Siemens had established a global platform for key account management and customer focus — *Corporate Development Siemens One*, which operated the AMPO. By 2011, this platform served top customers worldwide via more than 1,200 Key Account Managers. Siemens One facilitated collaboration among sectors, divisions, and regions via global and regional account teams plus market-specific organizations. Frequently, the thrust of this initiative was to provide customers access to the entire Siemens portfolio.

- People: Use the power of Siemens. To encourage lifelong learning, in fiscal 2011, Siemens invested more than €250 million in training and education. Siemens embraced diversity by employing 65 percent of the workforce outside of Germany; Siemens believed that diversity sparked creativity and strengthened Siemens' position in local markets. Integrity was central to Siemens culture: Dow Jones Sustainability Index (2011) ranked Siemens first in its industry for the fourth year in a row; Siemens also received the highest possible rating in the compliance category.

Key Account Management Practice — and Excellence — at Siemens

Historical Development. As a product-based industrial conglomerate, Siemens' traditional management approach was decentralization; Siemens delegated maximum decision-making power to individual sectors and divisions. These units operated in different markets (Exhibit 2); Siemens incentivized sector heads to operate as *global entrepreneurs* with *end-to-end business responsibility worldwide*. Sector heads sat on Siemens' executive committee and held seniority over countries and regions. Nonetheless, Siemens secured some perspective balance inasmuch key regional interests were also represented on the executive committee.

The global entrepreneur philosophy worked well in aligning R&D efforts with market opportunities. But some customers — especially large and globally active - had multiple contact points within Siemens. Interaction among global players was typically diverse and perceived from a 'silo' perspective. Both Siemens' and customer employees focused on their individual goals: hence, Siemens executives were interested in making it easier for customers to do business with Siemens. Sometimes, several different Siemens units contacted a particular customer regarding the same issue and vice versa.

Siemens started to address this situation during the 1990s, using programs that provided both a single touch point for interactions on a global scale (the so-called '*Mr. Siemens*') and local representatives that responded to the needs of customers' local operations. Whereas chief information officers (CIOs), served by the Siemens Information and Communications group, had originally asked for comprehensive global touch points, some machine builder-businesses like automotive had asked for local contact partners. Meanwhile, as part of the drive to produce profitable growth within sectors and divisions by sharing technological and sales and marketing knowledge, sector heads increasingly promoted the concept of joint account teams for key customers.[9] As global industry consolidation continued during the 2000s, and cost pressures increased, Siemens pushed forward with Key Account Program development, enjoying strong support from successive CEOs.

Siemens Modern Approach. Effectively implementing Key Account Management within such a large organization as Siemens required a structured program to serve customers and support Key Account Managers. Constantly driven by management and coordinated by the newly established AMPO, Siemens developed a clear, disciplined approach to account classification and selection. Siemens appointed three types of Key Account Managers: CAMs, GAMs, and RAMs.

Corporate Account Managers (CAMs) served customers with global reach that had important relationships across multiple Siemens' divisions. By 2012, Siemens had 144 Corporate Account Manager. CAMs were physically located near customer head offices; CAMs reported to a Market Development Board (MDB) and were legally managed by local management. (Exhibit 6 shows a full list of MDBs.) Based at corporate headquarters in Germany, each MDB was responsible for setting global strategy for a specific customer industry, like airports, metals and mining, or the power utilities. The evaluation process to select markets for MDB coverage was rigorous, including identifying potential for additional growth from a global, cross-sector strategic process. From 2005 to 2012, Siemens' MDB markets sales grew nearly triple Siemens' overall growth. In October 2011, responding to the urbanization megatrend, Siemens converted the *Cities* MDB into Siemens' fourth full Sector — *Infrastructure & Cities*.

Global Account Managers (GAMs) focused on global key customers with high potential for a single division. Customers in this classification were a more natural fit for Siemens' historic strategic thrust and entrepreneurial division-orientation structure. Within their divisions, GAMs worked across regional and country lines with local sales and operations teams so as to identify customer needs and build value offers.

Regional Account Managers (RAMs) addressed regionally focused or country specific customers, both for individual businesses but also those presenting cross-division opportunities. Siemens appointed more than 600 RAMs worldwide.

Exhibit 7 provides an overview of the role of each type of Key Account Manager. Exhibit 8 shows the crucial role Key Account Managers play in connecting customer organizations with the entire Siemens organization.

Siemens selected individuals for each type of Key Account Manager role based on previous experience. Most Key Account Managers had worked with Siemens for several years and had established a far-reaching network of internal contacts, plus a thorough understanding of Siemens and its extensive product portfolio. Whereas some positions required technical expertise that Siemens did not possess, Siemens found it overall more effective to recruit internally. To ensure continuity with key customers, but also avoid the pitfalls of long-term appointments, Siemens expected Key Account Managers to stay in their appointed roles for five to ten years.

Siemens offered Key Account Managers a broad range of on- and off-the-job training, comprising several educational modules that they completed within the early years of their tenure. Siemens taught Key Account Management techniques via Siemens-specific courses using internal tools, like creating account business plans within the global CRM tool during one course. The educational process immersed Key Account Managers in Siemens culture and terminology. The training program comprised five modules:

- Basic training. Applied to individuals appointed Key Account Managers for the first time or Key Account Mangers recruited externally. The focus was on the Siemens Account Development Process plus supporting techniques and tools.

- Modules one to four were for experienced KAMs. These modules focused on topics like internal and external collaboration, key financial concerns like CAPEX and value-chain analysis, plus enhancing project management and communication skills.

Siemens devised training content and concepts internally but external service providers conducted individual training sessions. Participants secured the title *Certified Siemens Key Account Manager* (CAM, GAM or RAM) by successfully completing at least two training modules, a terminology and concepts examination taken via the Siemens Intranet, a required level of practical experience, and a professional presentation highlighting a measurable real-world success.

In May 2011, Peter Löscher received the *Program of the Year* award for Siemens from the Strategic Account Management Association (SAMA) at its annual conference in Orlando, Florida. In accepting the award, Löscher stressed his conviction about the importance of being close to customers: "*Proximity to our customers is decisive for our business success. I myself spend more than half my time with customers.*"[10] For Siemens, the SAMA award was recognition of a decade worth of effort in developing a comprehensive, coherent, and accountable interface with customers. Exhibit 9 shows Siemens`view on the KAMs´ role as architect of structure in a sales team serving a key customer.

By fiscal 2012, Siemens top 100 customers accounted for 25 percent of all new orders; Key Account Management was involved with 40 percent of all new orders. Siemens was a recognized global leader in customer relationship management (CRM) and Key Account Management. Building upon the importance of game-changing megatrends like urbanization and globalization, Paulo Martinez was planning to extend account management programs to 67 cities, particularly in Asia.

Executive Sponsorship — a Crucial Element in Key Account Management

Consistent with its focus on Key Account Management, Siemens put in place the Executive Relations Program (ERP) to establish top-level relationships with senior executives at major customers. Each executive committee member sponsored customer-specific engagement strategies at several Siemens top accounts globally. Siemens regional leadership was similarly responsible for top regional key accounts. As Radeep Prahar, a corporate account manager based in Mumbai, India, put it: "*ERP fosters good relationships in the long run and on a global basis between the top management of Siemens and our customers. There is a lot of potential in the program as both do good business with each other. It is extremely useful for down-to-earth discussions about how we could collaborate in the future.*"

Executive committee member, Alex Amato, emphasized: "Our Executive Relationship Program (ERP) is a good program. It puts the focus on our key customers' needs — at the executive level. Formerly, key customers were lacking that direct relationship to the C-level. This is enriching for our company — as well as for us as executives sponsors - and drives our culture change within Siemens. "Customer focus is a board topic! Although Key Account Managers (KAMs) know best how to handle their key customers, we can now find out about their needs and requirements on a daily basis. KAMs are aware of what's going at their customer; they see their customers' needs, and identify opportunities — they help us truly understand our key customers. I consider this as a hands-off role, and I am always available for our key customers and KAMs whenever necessary. In addition to my accounts I will follow up proactively every quarter."

ERP ensured senior management took an active role in developing and implementing key account strategy. Topics particularly benefiting from executive involvement included joint development efforts for new technology; discussions went well beyond day-to-day interactions related to sourcing. Executive committee member, Adrian Carlisle, referred to one of Siemens' customers in the energy sector: *"Traditionally, they had had a lot of small companies as suppliers. For them, Siemens was a big company, which made them feel much more secure. Since starting our partnership, we have jointly engaged in pioneering activities on energy efficiency. After all, Siemens has a reputation for doing the right thing."*

Quite frequently, executive committee members would make sure that project teams evaluated alternatives based on indicators of sustainability, Siemens' guiding principle. Said Catherine Jankovic, a Key Account Manager based in the New York metropolitan area, *"The ERP program has a whole lot of value if the executive sponsor is truly part of the team. This way, he gets a thorough understanding of the issues we all face; and he is in a position to make sure we align every single step in the project with our overarching principles — such as sustainability. In addition to that, no one wants others coming into their space unescorted — it's often good to have an executive sponsor as that escort. And this is a lot more than meet the customer once a year, shake hands, exchange cards, have a nice dinner, and then walk away. Executives are on the team, they are no different than everyone else — they are expected to roll the ball as hard as everyone else. Although they may have a somewhat different view of the world, and a different level of dialogue, their role is no more or less important than everyone else's on the team. Everyone has input, and everyone's input is valid; but everyone is also responsible for driving issues to the next level, and that includes the executive sponsor."*

Jankovic continued, *"You need to continue to think about what's happening with your customers — by the time you read the news on the Internet, it's too late. This program enables discussions that you would never have in a day-to-day customer environment. It opens a lot of doors for us and we get into areas that we wouldn't otherwise be at. First and foremost it builds ownership of Siemens within the customer account. We would never ever have these opportunities were it not for that senior dialogue, establishing some type of advocacy for Siemens inside the customer's organization."*

CAMs served 55 of the 99 key accounts that had direct relationships with one of the ten executive committee members by mid 2012 — for example most of all large automobile manufasturers. GAMs served 30 customers; RAMs served 14 ERP accounts. Program guidelines suggested that the ERP contact would meet at least twice annually with appropriate customer counterparts.

A key task in setting up the ERP program was allocating executive committee members to specific customers. Many Siemens executives expected this to be a tedious and difficult process but, in fact, the matching process worked out smoothly for most accounts. Sometimes, personal relationships already existed — perhaps key Siemens and customer executives had attended school together or were each members of an organization or association. Such matches were quite natural, and professional aspects fit well with underlying personal bonds. A major success factor was the internal message that the global Siemens team serving a key customer received — the personal engagement and attention of the executive.

Some frictions emerged when two or more executives felt they should be the executive sponsors at a particular account. Matts Goetze recalled one incident when one executive asked another: *"You care for **my** customer?"* But even those situations were resolved rather easily. Siemens implemented a step-by step framework for guiding the matching process that resolved disputes on an impartial basis. Trust issues were always involved in determining who should care for which customer.

In another case, the executive believed his personal involvement with a particular customer would be inappropriate due to a conflict of interest. When the executive made the potential conflict transparent, the AMPO effected a change, and asked a colleague to engage with that customer. The matching framework included the following steps:

1. Assignment based on management responsibility for a particular executive (sector relevance or regional relevance)

2. Adjustment based on specific reasons per individual executive, like existing regular meetings between Siemens and customer executives in another association/organization

Once Siemens established the ERP program, it proved extremely useful for broadening the firm's appeal to customers that had been purchasing from Siemens in particular product areas for many years. Insights drawn from conversations among executives helped Siemens understand customer issues much more thoroughly: Catherine Jankovic reflected on a recent executive-level meeting with one of her most loyal accounts: *"We didn't really know them — we didn't know where they were going. Shouldn't we at least understand where they are right now and let them show us their roadmap, without any obligations? After just an hour's meeting everybody on the table saw tremendous opportunity for cooperating on a much broader scale. This would absolutely never have happened, had we not had executive dialogue going on."*

Executive sponsor Adrian Carlisle emphasized that *"Key Account Managers need to pull together knowledge and devise a package that can be executed. For example, a typical large-scale city needs to get millions of people from A to B through their public transportation facilities every day. That's exactly what the city council needs to get accomplished — they do not care about putting in place a specific subway train or bus. So that's what our Key Account Managers have to focus on as well. Obviously, there is a compensation issue — some KAMs might actually believe that these kinds of activities are diluting their business — they would rather just sell off a few subway trains."* Carlisle was not entirely happy with Key Account Managers performance on accounts he sponsored: *"Siemens needs better Key Account Managers, who can actually execute. Some would be way too terrified if they did not have executive committee support. They need to be fearless and see the opportunities — like Marcus Darabello, who just recently won the 'Siemens award in Key Account Management. Actually, people laugh when I say 'I work for Marcus' — but he truly has that kind of reach at both Siemens and his customer. Siemens has experienced a couple of disappointments, as KAMs do not always execute on leads my colleagues and I lay for them. We need to replace KAMs who are too weak for this job."*

Drawing on ERP success at the executive committee level, Siemens worked on initiating similar programs in Siemens geographic regions. By 2012, senior Siemens executives in more than 70 countries were involved in executive sponsorship programs, mostly operating on a national level. U.S. and German programs were particularly important because of these markets' size and importance to Siemens. Frequently, executives involved in country-specific programs played a critical role in supporting the top-level sponsorship program for global key accounts, especially when local issues could be addressed more effectively at a regional level.

As the ERP program grew and became institutionalized, executive committee members' engagement grew likewise. Siemens original expectation was that one executive would deal with five to ten customers. But due to strong executive buy-in, by 2012 the program involved 99 customers. Robert Traber sponsored more than 15 customers; Traber considered this commitment "about right." However, time requirements for external meetings, frequently including air travel and overnight stays, made it ever more difficult to actively drive focused interactions. Along with the growing number of sponsored accounts, once in a while the Account Management Program Office (AMPO) has been approached by KAMs asking for information in terms of results from i. e. informal-meetings between their Executive Sponsor and the customer (i. e. congresses) which the KAMs did not attend. Generally the rules of the program intended the Executive Sponsor to provide according feedback to the respective KAM what sometimes kept pending in the wake of tight schedules.

Jankovic said, "*My observation is they have too many customers — some of them have a dozen — especially since frequency of interactions is one of the important factors. Executives need to be connecting to their customers several times in a month in order to solve challenges and get through barriers; how can they do that — at the appropriate level of quality — for twelve or even eight different accounts? After all, they also have day jobs.*"

Key Account Managers differed on the required frequency of executive-sponsor discussions. Prahar stated: "*I think having a meeting at the top level once in six months is more than enough. You need to understand and learn what is the right amount of time to spend with each customer. Some people may welcome you every month, others may say once in twelve months is good enough for me. We need to prioritize based on this insight, and keep that balance. Of course, this has a lot to do with the local culture in a country as well.*" Matthias Krimmer, a Global Account Manager based in Northern Germany, put it this way: "*Less time spent on clearly defined objectives is better than more time wasted on fluffy conversations. Discussions should be short and focused, and take place in an intense way on just a few occasions.*" Adrian Carlisle stressed, "*With any meeting, you are taking your customer's time. So you better say something that makes their business better; just showing up is simply not enough.*"

Executive sponsor Alex Amato shared an example that demonstrated the impact ERP could have: "*For many years, we've partnered with New York City. Together with KAMs, we have mastered a number of challenges, and our focus on sustainability has been particularly well received here. Based on this, KAMs were recently advancing a project by which Siemens would have installed wind turbines at a very visible place in the city. This would have definitely raised awareness of clean energy in New York, and to them, it seemed to make perfect business sense. The ERP-framework ensured that we thoroughly reviewed project financials, under my guidance. The outcome was that the project in fact did not make sense for Siemens from a financial perspective, so we decided not to pursue it further. Generally, our relationship with New York City has strengthened due to the ERP. City officials consider us as a long-term partner in moving the city forward on its path towards sustainability. Just recently, we were invited to take part and exchange thoughts during the Annual Regional Assembly, hosted by the*

Regional Plan Association. Among the attendees were key people from both New York City and New York State; our company was the only business representative present."

Executive Relationship Program: The role of the Account Management Program Office (AMPO)

The AMPO was responsible for interacting with Siemens sectors and divisions about the program. The AMPO was also active in devising job descriptions for new Key Account Managers (in collaboration with human resources), evolving the training portfolio, and negotiating with employee representatives and unions to establish basic agreements on standards and procedures. Regarding the ERP program, the office was very involved in keeping the overall portfolio of sponsored key customers focused on the most promising ones.

Jill Hayden was responsible for the ERP within Corporate Development Siemens One. Her tasks included an annual review of the development of the program with executives and their back-offices and to support KAMs and their sponsors in their ongoing operations via activities like coaching Key Account Managers new to the program and central reporting.

Both Hayden and Goetze were very pleased with ERP's success. Each had worked hard over a considerable time period to drive the program, and ensured the entire executive committee provided support. They strove to enhance ERP's relevance to the executive committee such that ERP was frequently discussed among Siemens most senior executives. Without question, ERP was now considered a program of significant strategic importance to Siemens.

Hayden's key task was to review key accounts for potential inclusion within ERP. As Siemens executives became more familiar with the program, leadership group members started to offer Hayden suggestions for adding new customers. She viewed these suggestions in light of a set of predefined criteria:

- Strategic importance to the company, economically and technologically
- Mid-term growth potential
- CAM/GAM/RAM duly nominated
- Anticipated value-add of C-level engagement
- Purchasing presence across several regions
- Centralized purchasing in place

Under AMPO guidance, Key Account Managers produced account business plans (ABP) for each sponsored key customer annually. These plans detailed the approach taken by both Siemens Key Account Managers and executive sponsors in addressing each key customer, and indicated expected revenue growth and future developments. ABPs comprised several elements:

- Overview of customer business, including products and markets, and organization charts
- SWOT analysis and review of customer's industry and strategy
- Analysis of Siemens customer relationship status, including customer satisfaction ratings
- Executive relationship activities

- Share of wallet analysis; expected future development based on value-chain insights
- Potential new elements from Siemens portfolio
- Scorecard for measuring success
- Opportunities and next steps foreseen, decisions taken

Jankovic observed: *"A key part of the plan is an executive relationship map: Who is connected to whom? I need to make sure that my executive understands who he is connecting to, what that person's role is within the customer account, and why they are connecting; plus there has to be a calendar or schedule that is associated with that."* Executive committee member Adrian Carlisle confirmed: *"Before any customer meeting, we get a briefing statement. This helps us play just like Wayne Gretzky: we know where the puck is going to be next rather than where it was."*

Siemens drew market specific key insights, especially for anticipating future needs, from meetings among Siemens and customer executives. Customer executives talked about strategic insights regarding the future evolution of their businesses; KAMs translated these insights into activities designed to support the customer business effectively. Jankovic put it this way: *"We expect that our customer-side counterparts are going to provide some sort of coaching to us: Are we on point? Are we connected to the right people? Is there some other initiative within the account that we cannot see but that we should be sensitive to? Are any transitions occurring? Are there other political dynamics we need to be aware of? After all, it's not just sell to, it's sell with. You want your customer to co-validate your plan in order to make sure it makes sense from their business strategy standpoint. Sometimes, you can get all that validation in just one phone call."*

Carlisle emphasized: *"For the ERP program to be fruitful, there needs to be two beneficiaries: the customer and Siemens. Sometimes just a few minutes of pleasant conversation are sufficient to open new doors. You might find out about distractions from above and see stuff that is invisible from the outside. Siemens needs to* look at the world the customer CEO sees from his window. *Two years ago we helped one of our customers with an item-tracking issue we considered absolutely minor — it was definitely not a big sale for Siemens. But it did address one of the CEO's most pressing problems — plus it showed him new sides of the Siemens business, and this got our conversation around new technologies really going. Formerly, that customer had seen us as just another vendor — they might have had half an hour for a conversation with us and think: 'The sooner you're out, the better.' After we helped them reorganize their engineering, they started to realize the scope of what Siemens could really do for them. They now see us as a sparring partner that helps them in consulting and even implementing new production designs."*

Key Account Managers maintained a decisive role throughout the entire executive relationship process: They were responsible for advising executives on key issues to focus in meetings with specific customers; they were also responsible for communicating those issues where executive involvement was *not* needed. As Jankovic put it: *"You want executives from both companies to interact. Part of the dialogue should be 'tell me all your pain points, whether or not I can help solve them.' Maybe on one of them they will find something that is jointly rewarding, which they can do to align the two companies and make a better business offer."*

KAMs organized and led all meetings with executives, including preparation. Executives relied on KAMs' detailed insights and understanding of their specific customers. Executive committee member Adrian Carlisle complained about one particular follow-up conference call when this did not work out: *"There was no preparation whatsoever — it was just painful to have people talking about irrelevant issues. The KAM should have found out what the CEO wanted to talk about beforehand. We ended up in a situation where the customer brought in an expert and we could not really respond."* Mumbai-based Prahar felt that previous experience was crucial in succeeding in the KAM role: *"We need ten years at least before we can be truly effective. Executives' involvement should help on specific issues and advance the overall interpersonal relationship, and especially help transform Siemens into an even more customer-centric organization."*

Commenting on potential improvements to the ERP, Amato said: *"This is a good program for our company; however everyone involved, including us, as executive sponsors, can still improve. Key Account Managers have been great in organizing and preparing meetings — but sometimes they have a difficult time actually implementing and putting into practice what we agreed upon. Based on our setup, and particularly due to the newly created Infrastructure & Cities sector, there will be much less overlap, and KAMs will be able to fully focus on their accounts."*

Siemens introduced an extranet to facilitate communication between customers, KAMs and executive sponsors; this helped to sustain and develop strategic customer relationships. As Siemens product and key customer portfolios evolved their focus on social and environmental aspects, the ERP was instrumental in adding a new dynamic to that process. Strengthened account relationships at both KAM and executive levels allowed Siemens to better share its learning on sustainability issues with major customers, while simultaneously securing new insights from successful customer activities. A typical win-win example was a customer investing in new energy contracting and infrastructure, hence saving energy costs and improving its environmental record. Such partnerships enhanced both Siemens' and the customer's sustainability efforts.

The AMPO developed several approaches to evaluate the ERP. Key performance indicators were:

- Growth in order volume
- Growth of average revenue
- Customer recommendation (NPS)
- New portfolio elements

New relationships with key customer stakeholders
The AMPO also produced data for quarterly reviews; Löscher paid close attention to the ERP progress. Reports also included various detailed metrics broken down by executive committee member and sponsored account, including:

- Number of accounts per executive
- Orders growth per executive
- Additional information regarding upcoming projects and future development plans.

Siemens used Net Promoter Score (NPS) for tracking customer satisfaction and likelihood of each sponsored account to recommend Siemens, just as with all other key customers.[11] Each year, Siemens conducted 20-50 interviews per key customer so as to identify promoters, detractors, and individuals who were indifferent towards Siemens. Year by year results measured Siemens' evolution with a particular customer. Exhibit 10 shows the NPS calculation and Siemens' approach.

The AMPO used NPS to identify appropriate actions for improving Siemens' approach to serving customers. The main goal of NPS was to improve processes by leveraging customers' feedback. KAMs appreciated the NPS approach. One day Northern Germany based Krimmer told Goetze: "*There is that guy at my customer. He has been acting against us for years, but I never quite understood his issue. Yesterday I got the chance to talk things out with him based on his NPS feedback. NPS really is a great basis to improve our business relations.*"

Moving Forward

Despite his overall satisfaction with the Executive Relationship Program, Peter Löscher believed he and his team needed to reflect upon several issues related to ERP. Then they could decide what steps — if any — Siemens should take to optimize the program:

- Should there be more or less executive-sponsored customers?

- How much time should executives spend with customers annually, on how many occasions?

- In what way might the enormous success of ERP create pressure for the program to grow beyond the dimensions it was originally developed for — how may this affect both Siemens and sponsored accounts?

- Should the role of the Program Office be expanded and if so how?

- Does Siemens need new units or institutional structures? How about incentives?

- Do you have ideas for a slim debriefing-process between the Executive Sponsors and the KAMs in case of meetings limited to CxOs (i. e. conventions)?

ENDNOTES

1 Prepared by Christian Wallner under Noel Capon's supervision. Jacqueline Hitchfeld, Director Executive Relations, and Hajo Rapp, SVP Key Account Management and Market Development, provided significant assistance.

2 All names following have been disguised

3 www.siemens.com/history/en/history/index.htm

4 "The Task Facing Siemens," *The Economist*, 4 July 1992; "Sea Change at Siemens," *Management Today*, 1 March 1994.

5 *Siemens achieves record operating results. Annual Press Conference Fiscal 2011*, November 10, 2011, accessed via http://www.siemens.com/press/en/pressrelease/index.php on November 15, 2011

6 *Siemens 2012. The Company*, December 2011, accessed via http://www.siemens.com/press/pool/de/homepage/the_company_2012.pdf on January 3, 2012

7 *Strong End to an Excellent Year, Earnings Release Q4 2011*, November 10, 2011, accessed via http://www.siemens.com/press/en/pressrelease/index.php on November 15, 2011

8 *Siemens 2012. The Company*, December 2011, accessed via http://www.siemens.com/press/pool/de/homepage/the_company_2012.pdf on January 3, 2012

9 "It's payback time for Siemens' industrious unit chief," *Financial Times*, 13 Oct 1998.

10 www.siemens.com/press/en/pressrelease/?press=/en/pressrelease/2011/corporate_communication/axx20110561.htm

11 Net Promoter Score is a customer loyalty management tool. Several customer executives respond to a single question (0 to 10 rating scale: 10 = "extremely likely"; 0 = "not at all likely": "How likely is it that you would recommend our company to a friend or colleague?" Based on their responses, customers are categorized into one of three groups: Promoters (9–10), Passives (7–8), and Detractors (0–6). Net Promoter score (NPS) is percent Promoters less percent Detractors. NPS ranges from -100 (all detractors) to +100 (all promoters).

EXHIBIT 1: SIEMENS' MEGATRENDS

For more information on megatrends and Siemens' use of the megatrends concept for branding products and services:

Siemens Megatrends   http://www.youtube.com/watch?v=MwK-taIwNHs
Mastering the Megatrends   http://www.youtube.com/watch?v=BWXG-TsDAqc
Solutions for Sustainable Cities http://www.youtube.com/watch?v=z2nq-EsWacg

Demographic change and healthcare	Urbanization and sustainable development
All over the world, healthcare costs are already straining the financial resources of governments and insurance providers. In some industrialized countries, they now consume more than ten percent of gross national product — and the figure is rising. In the rapidly growing emerging and developing countries, healthcare quality is not improving as rapidly as inhabitants would like. That's why our challenge now is to boost the efficiency and affordability of medical services while improving the quality of individual patient care.	By 2050, the proportion of city dwellers will have risen to 70 percent — with a simultaneous increase in world population. Today's booming urban centers are making a major contribution to economic development. For example, 40 percent of Japan's gross domestic product is generated in Tokyo, while Paris accounts for 30 percent of all the goods and services produced in France. As cities increase in economic importance, their inhabitants are demanding a higher quality of life. Clean air, clean water, reliable energy supplies and efficient transportation systems are key needs.
Climate change and energy supply	**Globalization and competitiveness**
Innovations are the most effective means of combating the negative consequences of climate change — innovations relating to energy efficiency, power generation, power distribution and energy consumption. As a world-leading supplier of products, solutions and services for the entire energy conversion chain, Siemens is a pioneer in all these fields. Our technologies are enabling us to push the efficiency of fossil-fuel power plants, wind farms and solar power systems, develop smart power grids, boost the energy efficiency of production facilities and create energy saving lighting systems.	As the 21st century unfolds, the significance of national economies is declining. Business networks are becoming increasingly globalized as more and more companies compete internationally. To succeed in today's global economy, companies have to think and act internationally. We support customers in some 190 countries, and we've had operations in the BRIC countries for over 100 years. Our aim is to manufacture cost-efficient, affordable, high-quality, customized products all over the world. We can supply global customers with simple solutions worldwide — systems that can improve the lives of people everywhere.

Source: Siemens 2010 Annual Report

EXHIBIT 2: SECTORS AND DIVISIONS AS OF OCTOBER 1, 2011

Energy	Healthcare	Industry	Infrastructure & Cities
Divisions	**Divisions**	**Divisions**	**Divisions**
Fossil Power Generation	Imaging & Therapy Systems	Industry Automation	Rail Systems
Wind Power	Clinical Products	Drive Technologies	Mobility and Logistics
Solar & Hydro	Diagnostics	Customer Services	Low and Medium Voltage
Oil & Gas	Customer Solutions		Smart Grid
Energy Service			Building Technologies
Power Transmission			OSRAM [1]

1) In fiscal 2011, Siemens announced its intention to publicly list OSRAM and, as an anchor shareholder, to hold a minority stake in OSRAM AG over the long term.

EXHIBIT 3: SIEMENS' KEY PERFORMANCE INDICATORS, REGIONAL SPLIT OF REVENUE

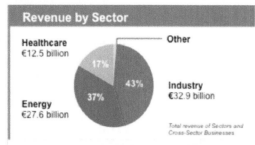

Revenue by Sector

Healthcare €12.5 billion

Other

17%

43%

37%

Industry €32.9 billion

Energy €27.6 billion

Total revenue of Sectors and Cross-Sector Businesses

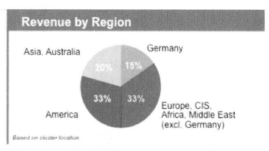

Revenue by Region

Asia, Australia

Germany

20%

15%

33%

33%

America

Europe, CIS, Africa, Middle East (excl. Germany)

Based on cluster location

Revenue and employees

100,000 — 500
Employees in thousands
80,000 — 400
60,000 — 300
40,000 — 200
20,000 — 100
Revenue in millions of euros
FY 1986 1990 1995 2000 2011

Key figures

Continuing operations (in millions of euros)	FY2010	FY2011
New Orders	74,055	85,582
Revenue	68,978	73,515
Income	5,974	9,242
Free cash flow	7,043	5,885
Employees	336,000	360,000

As of September 30, 2011

EXHIBIT 4: THE EXECUTIVE COMMITTEE

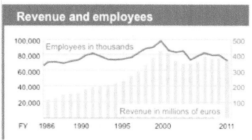

Peter Y. Solmssen (left) Corporate Legal and Compliance, Americas

Hermann Requardt (right) Healthcare

Joe Kaeser (left) Corporate Finance and Controlling, Financial Services, Siemens Real Estate, Equity Investment

Peter Löscher (center) President and Chief Executive Officer, Corporate Communications and Government Affairs, Corporate Development

Brigitte Ederer (right) Corporate Human Resources, Europe, Commonwealth of Independent States

Barbara Kux (left) Corporate Supply Chain Management, Corporate Sustainability, Global Shared Services

Michael Süß (right) Energy

Klaus Helmrich (left) Technology, Corporate Technology

Siegfried Russwurm (center) Industry, Corporate Information Technology, Africa, Middle East

Roland Busch (right) Infrastructure & Cities, Asia, Australia

EXHIBIT 5: EXAMPLE OF SIEMENS' "CORPORATE" ACCOUNT RELATIONSHIPS

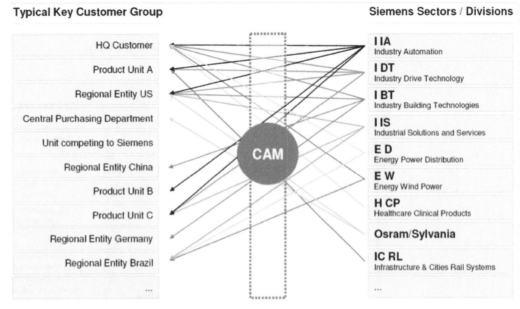

Source: Company data

EXHIBIT 6: SIEMENS' MARKET DEVELOPMENT BOARDS

Source: Company documents, as of June 30, 2012

EXHIBIT 7: ROLE AND TYPE OF KEY ACCOUNT MANAGERS

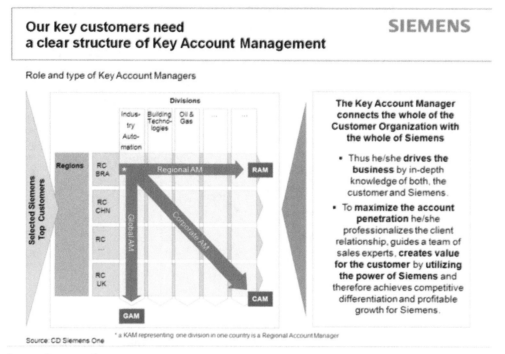

Source: Company documents

EXHIBIT 8: CONNECTING THE CUSTOMER ORGANIZATION WITH THE WHOLE OF SIEMENS

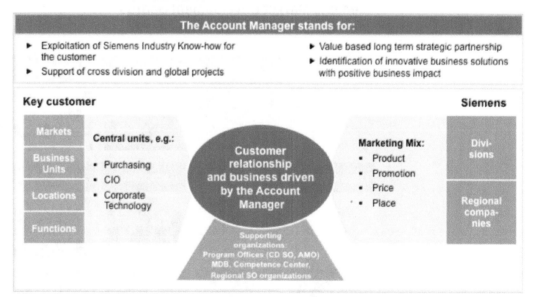

EXHIBIT 9: THE SIEMENS KAM AS ARCHITECT OF STRUCTURE

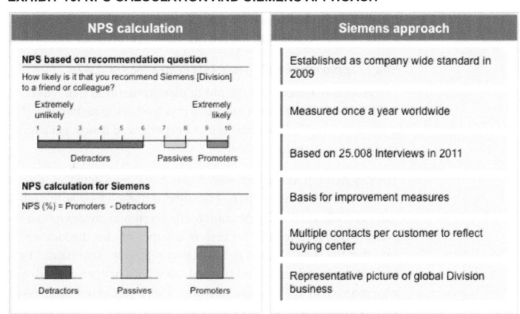

Source: Company documents

EXHIBIT 10: NPS CALCULATION AND SIEMENS APPROACH

NPS calculation	Siemens approach
NPS based on recommendation question	Established as company wide standard in 2009
How likely is it that you recommend Siemens [Division] to a friend or colleague?	Measured once a year worldwide
	Based on 25.008 Interviews in 2011
NPS calculation for Siemens	Basis for improvement measures
NPS (%) = Promoters - Detractors	Multiple contacts per customer to reflect buying center
	Representative picture of global Division business

Appendix

EXECUTIVE SPONSORSHIP: DISCUSSION WITH A GLOBAL ACCOUNT MANAGER

My name is Marcus Darabello. I am a global account manager with Siemens, based in Columbia, South Carolina. I graduated from Augusta State University (Georgia) with a bachelor's degree in industrial technology. I started my career with a small company now owned by a large competitor of Siemens. When I left in 1994, I was in charge of U.S., roughly $200m. Then I became vice president of sales for a medical company and later president of U.S. operations, reporting to the CEO. Siemens bought that company, and asked me to run its U.S. instrumentation business; I did that for six years. In 2002, I received an EMBA from the Darla Moore School of Business, University of South Carolina. Siemens appointed me vice president of service, a very tough assignment because I had to restructure the operation. After three years, in 2006, I became Siemens' global account manager for a major energy customer.

At Siemens, we really didn't have a defined executive relations program until Peter Löscher became CEO. Prior to that, Key Account Managers had seen executive interest; executives were sincere, they were interested, and they took on some activities with customers. The difference was that Löscher added structure and assigned particular responsibilities. This led to a real change in behavior and executive focus. Adrian Carlisle is the executive for the customer I work with. Adrian has very actively engaged with the customer, driven by Siemens' measurements. Adrian actually joined the executive committee after Löscher arrived; he and I have been involved with the energy customer for about three years.

How to approach executive relations in an effective way?

The process that Siemens One put in place recognized that we should not *jump into the pool at the deep end* — getting the executive involved in the customer and then *be in the water trying to achieve something*. The approach as I experienced it was: get a formula or recipe — or let's say structure — on how to start.

The Key Account Manager always has to have some detail on the customers's current situation, so when you talk with the executive, it doesn't look as though the account is not being managed. Hence, the Key Account Manager should always have a business plan in place for executives to review, and this review is important for the kick off. The next step is making sure that the business plan gets updated regularly. Anyone can look at the stock exchange and get an annual report and understand what's happening with a company, or how it's being perceived by the investment world. That's part of our business plan, but only one piece. Having much greater insight is critical to Siemens. To have a sound relationship with the customer, you have to understand your own position: Are you a supplier? Or are you are an advisor? And what is your overall scope? Of course, Siemens is extremely complex, because of its many businesses, so we can face a customer — or any large industry — in a variety of ways.

When Adrian and I first visited the account as a team, our approach had several key elements:

- What is the current status of our relationship?
- What are we supplying to them?

- What's our vision for the customer? And, most importantly:
- What is our strategy to achieve that vision?

Then we needed to make transparent what Adrian was going to do; what could be the purpose of having him on board. Adrian works extremely well. The first time I met him, I asked him a very open question: *"What do you expect as the executive sponsor — do you want to be involved only in C-level meetings, at the very high level, and talk to people who are on the board? Or do you want to roll up your sleeves and do some real work?"* His answer to me was equally interesting. He said: *"I only want to do what will be beneficial for the relationship between our companies."* Then I said: *"Ok Adrian, you have seen all the details of our business plan, our current relationship, our portfolio, our strategy, and my current actions. What we need to do now is make sure it will be effective."* So I laid out our first year plan for him and included specific contacts and meetings that we needed to do. The first thing Adrian showed was that he would do whatever was required to benefit the customer relationship. Adrian really worked hard, and that was noticed at the customer, particularly with the people we were calling on. They understood the importance of the executive attention they were getting. Some of the first comments we got back were that: *"There was full engagement during our meeting; we noticed that Adrian wasn't sitting down and working at his Blackberry, or checking e-mail. We noticed that Adrian gave us 100% of his attention; he wasn't interrupting and we didn't have changes at the last minute to accommodate his schedule."* It was a no-nonsense approach: we made an appointment, we had an agenda focused on what we wanted to do, and we got the desired results. That first year it truly was executive involvement at the working level, and this set the stage for us to later on have a deeper relationship with the customer.

Some Siemens people argued that we should not have Adrian in meetings that did not include the customer's CEO or senior VP. We actually did quite the opposite: we identified a significant project (€100 million) where Adrian could add value as the executive sponsor. This project definitely warranted attention of our C-suite. Adrian's responsibilities included attending regular meetings on behalf of the project, and to show Siemens' interest so that involved business units kept a clear focus. He made sure issues were communicated upward properly and quickly in both companies, and that we sought solutions in a team spirit. Adrian has visited the customer's plant three times, been involved in telephone meetings, and he keeps contact with the customer's senior sponsor. They have discussions and routinely seek information about what's going on, how teams are performing, or if any issues should be addressed. Executive sponsorship encourages, requires, or even forces project teams to pay special attention to the supplier-customer relationship. At the most recent onsite meeting, we were installing equipment that requires heavy construction: Adrian continued in his role. What's also important is longevity, to ensure some consistency. The people on the customer side are not changing all the time, so it would be terrible if we had too many changes on our side.

Siemens is a very large organization: 360,000 employees and many different internal structures. We have a lot of country presidents and CEOs, and lots of titles around the world — this creates challenges. There are always people that cannot be involved although they want to be. Siemens' Key Account Managers must be very careful to avoid the feeling on the customer side that we are just bringing in the "executive of the day." Prior to ERP, I never really had a sponsor, and we didn't make as much progress, but now there is consistency. When the Key Account Manager has a sponsor who is going to act for a period of two or three years at least, this is a big advantage.

Manage and guide your executive's relationships as well as your own time

I think Adrian appreciates that these relationships must be managed to some extent. Oftentimes I get requests that are not meaningful: People tell me: "*Adrian needs this; could you find that out.*" But then I realize that this is just someone's interpretation of what Adrian might want or need. We all have a boss and, to some extent, we try to perform properly according to their directions. But if the direction is wrong, you have to interpret the ambiguity to make sure you are doing the right thing. You have to navigate through those distractions and manage them even if things are out of control. There's an old saying: "*The harder you practice, the luckier you get.*" For me it means: I have been lucky, getting Adrian to stick around and keep fully engaged for all those years; but I have also been continuously optimistic and prepared in approaching him. Of course I can still do better and I don't want to get in trouble for not doing the right thing. But I also think people in positions like Adrian's or a country CEO want to be guided and directed in the right way, so they can be successful in their role.

As we continue our executive sponsored relationship within the customer, now we do have boardroom conversations. Both Siemens and the customer actively manage these conversations. The customer has assigned a person as my counterpart. We compare who is doing what in terms of executive relations; this could be many different things: a public speaking engagement on sustainability, business development for the customer inside Siemens' organization, the World Economic Forum, or individual meetings with executives — each of us has a reason for that kind of discussion. Now we actively manage boardroom discussions. We are able to tell each other what we shall be doing, who should be talking to the CEO, or that we want to go to the customer's headquarters. For example, if we were interested in a particular country's development (like China), our interests are two-fold: First, what is the country's economic and political development; second, we would like to be a local supplier to the customer and they would like to have some local business relationship with Siemens.

We try to avoid foo-foo meetings — meetings without any real agenda. Someone might say: "*We have to call on the customer's CEO to move things forward.*" Then we march into the CEO's office and we're not really sure about the agenda. It's a high level meeting so everybody is nervous, but business objectives are not clear and we just get stuck. I avoid those meetings; I just don't want unnecessary pressure. Just knocking at the CEO's door is extremely ineffective and the wrong use of the executive sponsor. If you want meaningful dialogue at the C-level, you must earn your way into the C-level suite. You have to pay attention to the necessary steps. Sometimes you can be opportunistic, if the C-level executive sees a real value proposition they need to discuss. But generally, it's not useful to talk to the senior executive to be successful on a particular project. I have never seen C-level executives decide anything with respect to a particular project. They set direction; they set strategy; they make approvals; but they have a lot of highly competent people that can make decisions in their own departments and areas. This is one of the biggest problems I've seen, the pressure to only talk to the C- level suite.

There has to be a real need, a real value proposition for meaningful discussion at the C- level. Usually, if people try and engage with high-level management to force a decision it's not going to happen. Keeping executives updated might help to get better decisions at a later stage, but you have to take a long-term approach. Do not stump the executive by linking the issue to his decision-making authority alone! If you want to get a decision at the C-level, you must approach the individual at the appropriate time. This can be during, before or after the project. But always avoid nailing them down on one single current issue, as they are the ones who may either back you or interfere with you once further decisions are required down the line. Keep your own actions decoupled from that person's decision, so you can take one independent action, like visiting the CIO, and still take another independent action related to the project.

Time has to be managed. Any appropriately managed time in front of the client is fantastic. If you are in front of somebody and it's not planned, that's detrimental. That exposure may actually hurt you. When the Siemens team gets together for a meeting -- we might be negotiating a contract — we need to get responses on particular issues. The more managed time you get, the better off you are. Anybody can take people out to lunch, without a defined objective; l could do that almost anytime I want, but that would bring up only my face time. You do not really accomplish anything and you are acting more like friends than business partners. In my opinion those relationships are dead wrong; customers don't have time for that. Customers don't want them — it won't be helpful. Nobody wants an inappropriate relationship. What they want is a professional relationship that is managed and accommodating. We do this now, so when I talk about getting access and having a relationship I mean that in a professional way. Today the time we spend with customers must be managed.

The ability to communicate is key

How has my role changed with the implementation of ERP? It really has not changed at all. We now have structure, and there is a different demand on the role. C- level people judge whether their Key Account Managers are good or bad based on their ability to communicate to them regarding customer needs. I imagine Adrian compares business plans on performance and long-term strategies from various leaders who run world-class companies like ours. A Key Account Manager must similarly be able to do. But having as sponsor a regional sales manager responsible for $10 billion sales versus the general counsel of a multinational, multibillion-dollar global company, is a very different challenge. Communication demand has increased with the ERP, but I don't see any change in my role as a result; it's the level of communication that's different.

We share our market growth objectives with the client; the client shares their goals with us, and what they would like to see in the relationship. You have to keep it manageable though, and that is not always simple. It's about how successful we are in key business objectives we both consider important. One metric is: "*It's easy to do business with Siemens*". We have an active team around that metric with identifiable targets. Sponsorship does make a difference: a lot of things happen more smoothly as a consequence. There is more effective communication between management and it's easier to implement inside Siemens. People know the customer is important and there is focus on them. For example, if we need resources to do a project and they say, "*No, we can't do it,*" then I can produce arguments based on executive sponsorship and a business case as to why we should spend to secure those resources.

There is benefit to both sides — and this may not even be directly related to a specific order for Siemens. When you look at the relationship globally, we have to make sure we are gaining what we want overall. Obviously the client understands that we want to gain market share as well as business growth; and every client has its own specific needs: lower cost or reliability, and they also want some business from us from being our customer. We measure those metrics; the executive relationship definitely has a positive impact on our client's growth also.

How do I make effective use of my time?

Starting from the big picture, I have to do some long-term business planning. Siemens has a CRM tool into which I load data and statistics related to my work. Certainly I need to understand financially where my account stands regarding its goals. That's going to require 20% of my time: I prepare account business plans, so I have to develop data, and integrate it into an understandable format so I can communicate with people around the world. I have to build spreadsheets and PowerPoint slides.

A major part of my time is internal communication about project objectives or executive updates and activities — say 10-15% of my time. Another key element is collaborating with the customer. We are both engaged in what items to drive forward; this leads to lots of meetings. People around the world are involved, including the executive sponsor. I manage all these objectives including business development on about three major topics in which the customer is interested. That should be three topics we are also interested in, and each has a team working on it. This coordination requires another 15% of my time.

And then there is direct activity with the customer: We work on projects they prioritize for us, and there is follow up communication. In terms of people that I could talk to or e-mail, who would know who I am, that's something like 450 individuals at the customer. At a minimum, this takes another 25% of my time via telephone, electronic communication, or face-to-face visits. Of course there are a many fewer face-to-face visits because that's expensive, but it's required and that's a lot of travel. In terms of annual travel, I go to Asia three times for about two weeks each time, about six trips to Europe, and to the customer's U.S. headquarters once a month.

I manage the 20% administration time pretty effectively, including priority interrupts on scheduled appointments. Finally, I dedicate a fair amount of time to personal development, like the three-day SAMA (Strategic Account Management Association) conference in San Diego. At a minimum, I go to one formal four-day training course annually organized by Siemens One, along with online training we're required to take. Personal development is crucial; it takes 5-10% of my time. Plus I have to deal with daily emergencies: I could spend the whole day on an airplane to China because of a face-to-face meeting with a local client with whom I was negotiating. I want to help her because she's a customer. When I go to a region, 50% of my time minimum is with Siemens colleagues, 25% to 30% with the customer, and 20% on administration.

SUMMARY TABLE: THIS IS HOW I SPEND MY TIME:

Activity	Portion of my time
Long-term business planning: CRM tool, spreadsheets, slides	20%
Internal communication: Project objectives, executive updates	10–15%
Collaborating with the account: Coordination of meetings & objectives	15%
Project work with the account, follow-up communication, travel	25%
Administration	20%
Personal development: Conferences, training	5–10%

What do I do in a typical day? In the morning I take care of emergencies, communications, and have telephone meetings. I dedicate the afternoon to updating my business plan, particularly since Germany is six hours ahead and I get fewer phone calls from colleagues in Europe. Time well managed is always going to help me get things done. A long time ago I learned to write down important things, until I do them; so I see how long I'm carrying something around. If it's there for three months, maybe it's not so important. This is true for any piece of paper and e-mails: I look at them and I do something about them right away, or throw them out. There's lots of communication today, lots of unnecessary e-mails, so I have to force myself to throw things away. If I don't do that, then I have to file them appropriately; maybe something is useful for a project in the long-term. Anyway, that's how I manage my day.

There's no way I could spend two months in the office and get all my administrative stuff done and my business plans; it's just not practical. There are major projects I would lose. I have a goal set for myself in the long-term; but I need to be in my home town with the customer at minimum every six weeks. I carry records of whom I meet during those days. I keep in touch with major business units, and we have formal relationship meetings, either annually or biannually. I carry reminders and have the discipline to work on them, as those meetings do require work. The executive sponsor will be there, so I put myself on a schedule to get all things done and force myself to complete that agenda. Then the client also gets used to that timeliness and is expected to do the same thing. They try to achieve things on their sides or demand to work with you, so it helps if you have that discipline yourself.

What are the characteristics of a top-of-the-class Siemens Key Account Manager?

Our goal always has to be top-of-the-class. Top-of-the-class Key Account Managers stick to the following philosophy: *Things don't happen to me; I manage how they happen.* This is absolutely crucial. What separates people who excel is that they manage the situation. Talking about executive relations, if the executive sponsor knows exactly what he wants and you don't, you are going to have a very difficult time. If you interact with that person, you are not going to make a good impression. Things don't just happen to a Key Account Manager — they must be planned. Key Account Managers must make decisions about what's important and what's not. You've got to be able to tell people — including your executive — what's important for them to do — and what's not. When they ask you for things that are not important, you have to go back and ask: *"Do you really need that?"* Not to focus on things that are the wrong priority is probably the number one key criteria. The challenge is not to be intimidated and to manage it.

The second thing is: You've got to have fun and enjoy doing it. When I came to Siemens, I was a 'big fish in a small pond': I was the general manager for instrumentation, reporting to the sector CEO — but that was a $140 million business. I managed 125 people then, before I became vice president of service, and had 500 people reporting to me in a business that was about $120 million. There are different roles and levels, and different challenges at Siemens. Today, I have direct communications with the highest level of management on both sides. My company expects me to be the one that can talk to those people on the client side, so qualifications become important. I already did that when I was running my own divisions and I continue doing it as I'm running this account. That's what converts people into top-of-the-class Key Account Managers: They must have certain capabilities.

Siemens has requirements for top-level Key Account Managers: You have to be able to speak several languages. I lived in Mexico and spoke Spanish in international business. I had a work visa and opened a company in Brazil. I have those experiences. I had to report to boards of directors on management performance. All those things now serve me well as a Key Account Manager. When I communicate to executives, I do so as if I am running a business. The ability to do that makes me a lot more successful.

I would never want to put anybody in a position where they are not successful. If that happens without me being involved, then there is a problem with the organization. My biggest criticism is lack of feedback; hence my inability to generate action. Everybody should understand we have a particular objective; the customer expects substantial results and they have their own objectives. Without feedback and follow-up, you miss opportunities. If two C-level people get together and discuss, that's valuable time and you, as the Key Account Manager in charge, should know what happened. Recently this has improved, but it's still an area that could absolutely be done better.

Very senior people oftentimes don't take action themselves and think they don't have to inform anybody. The further away you get from the initial contact, the worse it gets. For example, Adrian might have an offsite meeting with somebody, and they agree on three different topics. Usually he turns around and informs me as well as two or three other people, each of whom needs to do something. As it gets further away from that original contact, communication deteriorates. I took the time and prepared the original briefing, I put three topics on the table that needed to move forward, so I should know if anything happened. If not, it's unsatisfactory; it might be just a waste of time or even make things worse. People seem to be afraid to say that nothing happened. Interaction with Adrian is really genuinely adding value. He is open to supporting and learning and this has made a big difference.

CPSIA information can be obtained at www.ICGtesting.com
Printed in the USA
BVOW10s0702090115

382589BV00002B/2/P